FAITH POSTURES

CULTIVATING CHRISTIAN MINDFULNESS

A Testament of Devotion
Thomas Kelly

"Listening"

Smyth & Helwys Publishing, Inc.
6316 Peake Road
Macon, Georgia 31210-3960
1-800-747-3016
©2009 by Smyth & Helwys Publishing
All rights reserved.
Printed in the United States of America.

Library of Congress Cataloging-in-Publication Data

Sprink, Holly.

Faith Postures : cultivating Christian mindfulness / by Holly Sprink.
p. cm. Includes bibliographical references.
ISBN 978-1-57312-547-5 (pbk. : alk. paper)
1. Spiritual life—Christianity. 2. Christian life.
I. Title. BV4501.3.S6647
2009 248.4—dc22 2009038048

Faith
Postures

CULTIVATING CHRISTIAN MINDFULNESS

Holly Sprink

What we say about God is always incomplete.

But when the Complete arrives,

our incompletes will be canceled.

(1 Corinthians 13:9-10, *The Message*)

Acknowledgments

Thanks so much to all of you who took the time to proofread this book with me, either in the earliest stages when this project was just a hobby or in the final editing phases. Thanks for your willingness to work through ideas as well as mechanics.

Thank you to my church families at Columbus Avenue Baptist Church, First Baptist Church of Woodway, and First Baptist Church of Blue Springs. Thank you also to the faculty at George W. Truett Theological Seminary. So much of me is made up of the things I learned from all of you.

Thanks, Leslie, for helping this first-timer through the process. You've graced me with your gift of kindly making all "the crooked straight and the rough places plain," in the text itself and in this process.

Thanks, Ashley, for your support on this project, and for rewriting and altering so much of my life story with your friendship.

Thanks, Mom and Dad, for encouraging me to read, write, and go to seminary. Thanks for all the Terrific Tuesdays.

Lucy, thanks for being so excited about my project with "Smiff and Hello-wys" and for letting me tell stories about you. God is shaping you, and I can't wait to see how and for what.

Matt, thank you for telling me I'm beautiful when I'm sitting in front of the computer with my fleece pajamas on and my hair pulled back. Thank you for recognizing and enabling Christ in me. I love our life together and I love you.

Contents

Part I: Learning the Art

Introduction 3

1. Noticing and Responding 7

2. Noticing Our (God-repaired) Selves 13

3. Noticing God's Reality 19

4. Noticing Immanuel 25

5. Noticing the Advocate 33

6. Noticing When We Obstruct Christ 41

7. Noticing World Family 47

Part II: Realignment

Introduction 59

8. The Posture of Creative Responsibility .67

9. The Posture of Expectancy in Worship .73

10. The Posture of Coping . . . and Hoping 79

11. The Posture of Hospitality: The Interpersonal Level 89

12. The Posture of Hospitality: The Corporate Level 95

13. The Posture of Contentment 103

14. The Posture of Peacemaking 109

15. The Posture of Sharing 117

16. The Posture of Tolerance 125

17. Conclusion: The Posture of Love 131

Part I

Learning
the Art

Introduction

Pos·ture *n.* **1** the position or carriage of the body in standing or sitting; bearing **2** such a position assumed as in posing for an artist **3** the way things stand; condition with respect to circumstances [the delicate *posture* of foreign affairs] **4** an attitude of mind; frame of mind.[1]

I take a yoga class once a week. Every Tuesday, while I'm balancing on one leg in Tree Pose (I seem to be more of a weeping willow) or hanging upside-down in *Uttanasana,* my teacher tells the class how each pose, when practiced regularly, will improve our mental and physical well-being. Certain poses are good for strengthening the back; others are great for relieving tired legs and so forth. She even said one time that Headstand and Shoulderstand, the king and queen of all yoga poses according to B. K. S. Iyengar, are "life-transforming poses." The list of ailments these two poses help is long, relieving everything from migraine and digestive ailments to, my personal favorite, irritability. I smiled through my Shoulderstand during class one day when I heard that one. I imagined myself telling my husband, "I'm sorry, honey, the baby is crying, the dog is barking, and you talking to me about the bills is making me feel a little bit irritable right now. I'm going to do a quick Headstand and then we can talk, okay?"

I have to admit that I was pretty skeptical when my first yoga teacher started talking up yoga as a holistic health measure. It sounded like another one of our human efforts to make x + y = z, to give a problem an easy answer. "Just stand on your head for three minutes a day and all your problems will float away!" Sure. But class after class, year after year, I keep going back. I've had different teachers with different styles, and each class and its members seem to have a different story. Their stories are amazing, but their lives are more so. Twenty-, thirty-, forty-, fifty-, sixty-, and seventy-year-olds gathered into one small room, challenging themselves physically and pushing themselves to be mindful mentally. Age is meaningless in the room, as are weight, color, status, and gender. Some who are old by newsstand standards can stand on their heads away from a wall for ten minutes at a time. Some who are overweight according to the opinion column have the most amazingly flexible hamstrings. Some who would be called beautiful by the box office have stiff spines. The variety spans stages of life, stages of flexibility, stages of wisdom. These people are different from the spandex-clad perfectionists in yoga videos and magazines. My classmates understand that life is so much more complex, that x + y doesn't always equal z.

As I listen to what the teachers and students are saying, over time I've discovered something. The teachers and students are not saying, "Here's the magic trick to cure your most annoying health issues." What they are saying is, "Here's a posture to assume when you're feeling misaligned." And when, over time, your hamstrings let you hang and your trapezius muscles aren't so tight, you realize that through devoting yourself to mindfulness, the desired postures come more naturally. You begin to see progress over time in specific ways. You can touch your toes when you couldn't before. You realize that by sitting up straighter at the computer, with your head and neck extending from your spine as in Mountain Pose, you relieve that nagging neck pain. You find you'd rather not stuff yourself at the lunch hour because you recognize such a meal's effects on your body by 3 p.m. It's not that the postures themselves immediately relieve pain the first time you do them, but that you develop your own awareness of how you're truly meant to be in alignment, physically and mentally. When you practice the postures, you learn to recognize when you're not aligned and how to correct yourself. Over time, the promised benefits *are* realized, and you notice them because you've been mindful all the while.

A question I like to ask my husband each day is, "What did you notice today?" I love this question because of the range of answers you receive when you ask it. It's more personal than "What did you do today at work?" I think my question secretly annoys Matt, but he's a phenomenal husband who plays along anyway. Once when I asked him, he had noticed an abandoned robin's nest. Another day, he had spotted a bunch of helium balloons that was floating up unnoticed by the used-car salesman who had just tied them to a car. One time he told me how he noticed the way someone belittled his work and how that made him feel. Some days, he'll ask me this question, and I'll ramble on for thirty minutes about something beautiful our daughter did that day. Other days, I'll say, "I haven't taken the time to notice anything today." Noticing aspects of our world and lives takes practice. It takes a deeper level of awareness than we normally use. Instead of plowing through our schedules, scattering shrapnel of voice mails and sticky notes everywhere, what if we took extra care to be mindful, matching up the way we *say* we want to live with the way we are actually living?

I'm not a football player, but I've watched enough Kansas City Chiefs games in my life to know that winning teams don't simply begin the game with a book of plays they all agree upon and then carry them out one by one until time runs out. A football game is a set of complex interactions. The players have to watch the game themselves, noticing who is in position and who has forgotten the plays. The coaches have to watch the game, making sure the offensive line provides protection and making sure the defense holds. Men with headsets way up in glass boxes watch the game, noticing what plays are effective and ineffective against the opponent. In the end, your team could have the most amazing playbook of all time, but if it doesn't notice when its game-day play fails to match the playbook and then doesn't make the necessary adjustments to reconcile the two, the playbook becomes meaningless. If your team isn't willing or able to adjust itself when it is misaligned or when it needs to respond to a particular situation with an opponent, it probably isn't going to have many notches in the "W" column.

In the biblical letter to the Roman believers, the Apostle Paul warns the Christ-followers against living life unaware. "Don't become so well-adjusted to your culture that you fit into it without even thinking," he writes. "Instead, fix your attention on God. You'll be changed from the inside out. *Readily recognize what he wants from you, and quickly respond to it.* Unlike the culture around you, always dragging you down to its level of immaturity, God brings the best out of you, develops well-formed maturity in you."[2] A life of faith is not something we float through on a cloud unaware; it is the mindful process of letting God change us, letting him develop our spiritual sensitivity toward the things of God and his kingdom.

As we begin to learn the art of noticing, to observe our own lives and the ways God interacts with us, we are better able to recognize and respond to him. We see the things in our lives he puts before us, we understand what he's asking of us. Just as in yoga, we begin to notice the ways our attitudes and actions are misaligned, and we see the negative effects of our sin. We take steps toward God, letting him re-create us. We begin to see there are certain *postures*, or attitudes of mind, according to Webster, that we assume as God transforms us into who he created us to be.[3]

I began thinking about faith postures one day as I found myself wishing there were yoga poses for my not-so-physical problem areas. "It would be nice, Lord," I prayed, "if every time I noticed myself speaking rudely or conveying something I don't mean through my tone of voice, I could assume a posture that would help me stop." He said, very simply, "There is such a pose. You take your top lip and press it tightly against your bottom one, holding them both there firmly until the desire to be rude goes away."

There are no quick, easy fixes, in yoga or in our lives of faith (hence the word *faith*). However, I believe God asks us to be aware, to practice the art of noticing God's transformational work in our lives. He gently and lovingly realigns us, guiding us into postures of faith that reflect his love. We Christ-followers claim to be the people of God, to live lives that reflect who our God is, and yet many times we are wholly unaware of the small choices we make daily that show him to be completely other than divine. How many ailments do we unknowingly cause ourselves and our God because we are unwilling or unable to notice? We have not developed the art of noticing. We must learn to be still, to listen, to be mindful, not only of ourselves, but of the One outside ourselves. In developing the art of noticing and practicing the postures of our faith in God, we begin to realize the spiritual health we yearn for.

And yet, even still, as we become mindful of who we are, who God is, and how that knowledge affects the way we live, there is still more in the equation. We are not able to make x + y = z, no matter how hard we might strive. The height of mindfulness is meaningless without the stirring of God's grace. In a life of faith, there are ultimately no self-help programs. Come, Lord Jesus.

Notes

1. *Webster's New World College Dictionary*, 3rd ed., s.v. "posture."

2. Romans 12:2, *The Message*. Through the rest of the book, I'll use *The Message* translation unless otherwise specified. This isn't a statement on Bible translations; it is simply the translation I was reading devotionally while I was writing this book and the one that inspired some of the illustrations and connections.

3. *Webster's*, s.v. "posture."

Chapter 1

Noticing and Responding

Everything (and I mean, precisely, everything) we do is a
response to God's first work, his initiating act.
—Eugene Peterson[1]

One of my favorite authors is Mark Twain. I come by this naturally, since anyone who grows up in Missouri like he did gets a good dose of him by the fourth grade. His great legacy for American fiction is the way he communicated truth through humor, what he called humanity's most effective weapon. Somehow he was able to size up almost any situation and relate it in a way that made you laugh first, pause, and then say to yourself, "Ouch."

He seemed to see through the self-righteousness humans put on, saying things like, "Be good & you will be lonesome,"[2] and "Always do right. This will gratify some people & astonish the rest."[3] Twain's audiences enjoyed themselves while they were with him, meanwhile soaking in his observations of the world they all knew.

However, it is not merely Mark Twain's humorous truth telling that made him a writer and speaker of such renown; it is also—and maybe more so—his ability to absorb American life. Ken Burns's documentary on Twain's life calls it Twain's "fascination with noticing" that began in childhood. This habit of noticing all that was around him served him well during his youth, when he worked as a steamboat pilot. Twain had to notice the difference between ripples on the water that were caused by wind and ripples that were caused by some unseen hazard hidden beneath the water's surface. "He was an enormous noticer," says writer Ron Powers. "He was a prodigious noticer. He was always noticing whether people had their hands in their pockets or not, or what was in their pockets. He was noticing manners of dress, the way people held themselves. He was noticing affects and pretenses."[4] He observed and absorbed life, which enabled him to communicate aspects of American culture unlike any other author and speaker. "The Mississippi became for Mark Twain his Harvard and his Yale," says Twain scholar Hamlin Hill. "He announced that every character he had ever written, created in his literature, he had met on the Mississippi River."[5]

Mark Twain felt that life was something to be explored, pondered, absorbed, and savored. As humans, it is imperative that we live life in such a way that we *give ourselves time to observe what is going on around us*. We must learn the art of noticing if we are to understand what it is to be fully human. This practice helps us realize and appreciate that we are not solitary lives around which the world revolves, but instead part of many complex systems in this life. Taking time to absorb people, places, objects, and the histories they each possess allows us to be fully present in life's situations instead of rehearsing past difficulties or projecting future worries. Noticing the details of our places in the world and in history allows us to draw truth out of our daily routines and act on it. Practicing this art of noticing encourages us to recognize and cultivate every ounce of beauty and love we observe, involving us in what it means to be truly human.

However, the art of noticing is not merely a sensory experience that gives us scientific knowledge or measurable data. We also absorb important aspects of life that affect us even though they cannot be seen or measured. Consider what extra knowledge we draw from the tone of someone's voice. Think of the different ways touch communicates meaning. Has your sense of smell ever triggered a memory your mind wouldn't have recalled? While it would be easy to differentiate between the visible and invisible information we take in, such a dichotomy is ultimately false; in reality, both our visible and invisible observations grant us a more complete understanding about the world and our place in it. Mark Twain said, "The common eye sees only the outside of things, and judges by that, but the seeing eye pierces through and reads the heart and soul, finding there capacities which the outside didn't indicate or promise, and which the other kind couldn't detect."[6] We realize, then, that this art of noticing must encompass both the visible and invisible aspects of life.

The spiritual word for the immeasurable aspects of our world that we take in is *revelation*, a word that in its Greek form suggests an unveiling of that which is unavailable to the natural senses.[7] This word has religious baggage, but here, we are simply talking about aspects and truths about life that are revealed to us. In Christian thought, it is believed that the things we know about life are not taken in simply by human effort, but that a benevolent God graces us with these understandings. Theologian A. J. Conyers says this idea of revelation means "this disclosure is not a neutral or impersonal event, but its character is 'God seeking man.' It is not gained by human powers of perception, but is a divine gift."[8] When Christians answer the question, "How do we know what we know?" we do not affirm our limited human conclusions but instead affirm God's grace as he initiates our understanding of life all around us.

Through the practice of this art of noticing, then, we are graced with the chance not only to experience life at its fullest, but also to know something of God. We have the opportunity to receive from God, not strive after him, because of his willingness to initiate a connection with us. Theologian Abraham Joshua Heschel said, "This is at the core of all biblical thoughts: God is not a being detached from man to be sought after, but a power that seeks, pursues, and calls upon man. The way to God is a way of God."[9] What does this ultimately tell us? It frees us from humanity's eternal struggle to strive toward God. It tells us that our ability to know God is not dependent on our understanding or virtue, but on God's desire to relate to us and to have us relate to him.

This particular truth is pure grace, uncovering for us the ultimate reason we should practice the art of noticing: so we can notice and respond to God. We don't work at the art of noticing so that we can find all the pieces to life's puzzle, reaching some state of consummate wisdom. We're not trying to gather clues like Sherlock Holmes in order to understand the meaning of life. We're not trying to be the first to point out truth to others so we can be know-it-alls, and we're not trying to gather information we can manipulate for our purposes. Rather, *we learn to notice so that we can respond to God's invitation to know something of him and how he works in the world.* Romans 1:19-20 says, "The basic reality of God is plain enough. Open your eyes and there it is! By taking a long and thoughtful look at what God has created, people have always been able to see what their eyes as such can't see: eternal power, for instance, and the mystery of his divine being." While people the world over have myriad ideas about how to practice Christianity, at its heart, the Christian faith is simply noticing and responding to God. We notice who God is, we absorb his transforming work in the world and in people, and we respond to him in faith and belief.

Consider how these ideas come to life in a conversation recorded in John 3 between Jesus and Nicodemus, a prominent leader in a Jewish sect.

Nicodemus comes to Jesus, albeit in the middle of the night, to talk about the things he's noticed about God. "Rabbi," he says, "we all know you're a teacher straight from God. No one could do all the God-pointing, God-revealing acts you do if God weren't in on it." Jesus congratulates Nicodemus on his perceptiveness, telling him that the people who will see the truth of this life—God's kingdom—must be born a second time, reborn in a spiritual sense. Nicodemus trips over the biology. "What are you saying with this 'born-from-above' talk?" he asks.

Then Jesus reminds Nicodemus, and us, that we don't birth ourselves. We don't have anything to do with the miracle of our own lives; we only take note of what is happening to us physically and respond to the creative act of love that brought us into being. We are born. Jesus says the process is the same with the spiritual side of our lives: God's love goes before us. *We don't have to orchestrate our own spiritual rebirth; we simply notice the love of God, respond to it, and experience the beginning of new life.* "Let me say it again," Jesus says. "Unless a person submits to this original creation—the 'wind-hovering-over-the-water' creation, the invisible moving the visible, a baptism into new life—it's not possible to enter God's kingdom. When you look at a baby, it's just that: a body you can look at and touch. But the person who takes shape within is formed by something you can't see and touch—the Spirit—and becomes a living spirit."[10]

We notice and respond to God's initiative, and this brings with it wholeness and life. We who follow Jesus need to live in this humble knowledge and practice it before others. It's grace that brings our births about, not something we do. How much more compassion would fill our lives—for others and for ourselves—if we continually renewed our infant's response to God's re-creation of us? How would our lives be different, fuller, if we took time each day to notice in humility the Spirit birthed in us? May the God who took initiative to grant us his Spirit through his Son aid us as we begin learning and practicing this art of responding to him, this art of noticing.

Learning the Art of Noticing
1. Give yourself time to observe what is going on around you today. Find a few minutes during the day or at the end of the day to notice your surroundings.
2. Voice a prayer of thanks to God for his willingness to initiate a connection with us.

Notes

1. Eugene H. Peterson, *The Contemplative Pastor: Returning to the Art of Spiritual Direction* (Grand Rapids: Eerdmans, 1989) 61.

2. Mark Twain, *Following the Equator*, 1897, quoted by R. Kent Rasmussen, ed., *The Quotable Mark Twain* (Chicago: Contemporary Books, 1997) 114.

3. Mark Twain, *Note to Young People's Society, February 16, 1901*, quoted by Rasmussen, ed., *The Quotable Mark Twain*, 238.

4. In Ken Burns, *Mark Twain: A Film Directed by Ken Burns*, VHS, Florentine Films and PBS Home Video, 2001.

5. Ibid.

6. Mark Twain, *Personal Recollections of Joan of Arc*, www.twainquotes.com, 7 October 2008.

7. A. J. Conyers, *A Basic Christian Theology* (Nashville: Broadman & Holman, 1995) 11.

8. A. J. Conyers, *A Basic Christian Theology* (Nashville: Broadman & Holman, 1995) 11.

9. Abraham Joshua Heschel, *God in Search of Man: A Philosophy of Judaism* (New York: Farrar, Straus and Giroux, 1955) 198–99, quoted in A. J. Conyers, *A Basic Christian Theology* (Nashville: Broadman & Holman, 1995) 17–18.

10. John 3:5-6, *The Message*.

Chapter 2

Noticing Our (God-repaired) Selves

May I know you, may I know myself!

—St. Augustine[1]

Sometimes I mistakenly read the Bible like a Jane Austen book. Life seems so simple in *Pride and Prejudice* or in *Sense and Sensibility*, the good people are good, the bad people are bad, and everyone knows who is who. Someone might come over from the dark side from time to time, or vice versa, but overall, things are nice and neat. The people in Jane Austen's books have astounding self-knowledge; they seem to *know* whether they're good characters or bad characters before the story begins. This is convenient because they can continue to do good or evil for the rest of their lives and fulfill their purposes in the story. No one seems conflicted about who he or she is—or who he or she is *supposed* to be.

When I read the Bible, sometimes I catch myself thinking of its stories in a similar way. The people I read about seem to have it all together. They seem to know who they are and discern their purposes on earth as if God had inserted microchips containing this information into their brains at birth. After all, they lived in "Bible Times," right? Many of them had physical encounters with God or interacted with Jesus. Surely that gave them an edge in figuring out their lives and what they were doing here in the world.

The thing I routinely forget as I read the Bible, however, is that these people were human. These people were not the created characters of the writers. They were not fabled placeholders that represent right and wrong. We cannot read the Bible this way, as we might read Jane Austen, without serious misinterpretation. The Bible is not the story of God's interaction with fictional Everyman and Everywoman. It is a collection of stories of God's encounters with humanity. These recorded lives were not prototypes. While we can learn much from them, these lives were not airbrushed cover models that God put on the cover of *Healthy Christian Man* or *Ideal Godly Woman.* These were humans. They journeyed. They learned.

Whether I read about it in the Bible or try to figure it out in my own life, this God-humanity interaction is hard for me to grasp. While I don't know all there is to know about the God side of biblical interaction, I know about the human side because I know myself. Or maybe I should say I know my own *lack* of self-knowledge. I know what it is like to wake up some days with insecurities, to wake up completely scattered and in need of integration. Some days I awaken to a thick, wet fog that obscures my sense of purpose in life. I am the opposite of a Jane Austen character. If the people in the Bible were the least bit human as *I* am human, they, too, must have experienced this conflict, this struggle to find meaning and purpose in our broken humanity. The people in the Bible, even those who had an encounter with God, Jesus, or one of their messengers, didn't immediately become fully and consistently integrated to the purposes of God. They didn't receive letters in the mail saying, "Hello, this is God. I would like to tell you why you are on this earth. I would also like to explain your character traits and the reasons I have given them to you. Further, I am going to explain your purpose in life and the exact role you are to fulfill by the time you die. Here goes . . . ."

These humans in the Bible had to notice their redeemed selves. They consistently had to trust how God was reshaping their broken humanity into integrated, God-glorifying life. Look at the disciples, the ones closest to Jesus. They worked, played, ate, and traveled with him. They messed up. They shipped out at times and, on occasion, they shaped up. Even those closest to Jesus didn't immediately become fully purposed, whole super-people. They had to learn to trust God's process of reinventing their lives as they followed Jesus. Even with the opportunity to encounter God and his Son in miraculous ways, they still had to take time to discover how God was reshaping their lives.

We, too, need to notice our redeemed selves. We need to believe firmly that, though we begin as selfish, imperfect characters in this divine comedy, God can redirect our purpose toward good. Believing this, waking up each day with this assurance, takes practice. Leaning into God's reinterpretation of each day in our lives takes focus and repetition. We have to follow the examples of those we read about in the Bible; we need to interact with God and, in doing so, notice the ways he is re-creating us. We must observe the quiet ways he is challenging us to leave behind our constricted understanding of life and breathe deeply of the beauty in his purposes for us—and we need to do this *each day*. This kind of self-knowledge is not a single enlightenment-like event. Conversion of our views of self in light of God is continual. We daily have to take the time to notice and trust in who he is in order to understand who we are. The book of Romans assures us that God's Spirit will fill each moment of our lives if we notice and trust the way he is repairing our humanity. "Those who trust God's action in them," says Romans 8:5, "find that God's Spirit is in them—living and breathing God!"

The biblical account of John the Baptist can teach us how to notice and lean into our God-repaired selves. John would have been a perfect Jane Austen character because he certainly had the "good-guy-who-has-it-all-figured-out" credentials. John had amazing encounters with God and his Son, Jesus. After all, he was Jesus' cousin, and he even leapt in the womb when he was near Jesus, virtually pointing toward the Christ from conception. An angel who visited John's father confirmed that John was to be special. What more could you want as far as credentials go? John must have immediately known that he was to be the one prophesied in Isaiah 40:3, the voice who would make straight in the desert a path for God. How nice for him to know his whole purpose—his true, God-given role—from the beginning.

But what else do we know about John? He didn't follow in his father's footsteps by signing up for the Jewish priesthood. He was religious, one could say, but in his own wild way, living an ascetic lifestyle in the desert. He rebelled against traditional Jewish life, rebuking his people with a scorching "Repent!" Then there's that troubling story about John later in life, when he sent one of his followers to ask Jesus if he really *was* the one who would re-create their lives. John wanted to know if he'd goofed up, if he'd been pointing toward the wrong person all along. He wanted to know if his efforts would matter for good or for evil.

What does this more complete picture of John the Baptist tell us? It tells us that John was human. It tells us that people then and people now consistently have to ask God to reinterpret and reinvent their humanity for his purposes. It tells us we have to trust in the ways God has redeemed and repaired our lives. In the first chapter of the book of John, priests and Levites asked John humanity's ultimate question: "Who are you, John? What is your purpose on this earth? Are you one of the good guys or one of the bad guys?"

What a question, especially when we realize that John was as human as we are, one piece of broken humanity who struggled to trust in God's repair work in his own life, as we all do. John wasn't sure of his purpose in God's grand drama. God had not cast a play and announced to the world that "John the Baptist will be reading the role of the Voice in the Desert found in Isaiah 40:3."

Yet, John used that verse to tell the Pharisees who he was. Why did he do that? How did he have the faith to believe in God's leading in his life? By using this Scripture to explain himself and his purpose to the Jews, John—unintegrated, rebellious John—dared to think God could use him to prepare people's lives for the ways Jesus would work in them. John recognized his humanity and, at the same time, hoped that the way God had moved him to live and teach would somehow point to the One who was to reveal God in human form. He dared to believe that who God challenged him to be and the lifestyle to which he was called would actually play a part in the grand interaction between God and man. He did not know for sure if he would land a part in this drama, but he declared in faith his willingness to accept a role.

What does this mean for us? When we wake up in a conflicted funk, when we're bummed about who we are, or when we're missing the point to life, what should we do? Do we give in to our insecurities and disengage from life? Do we downshift into maintenance mentality? Do we simply get through the day until we can crawl back under the covers? What practical things can we do to notice and trust God's activity?

First, I believe we can welcome God's reconciling activity in our lives. This means we notice, maybe for the first time, the way God reaches out to reconcile us to himself. He took the initiative to heal our broken humanity by becoming humanity himself in the person of Jesus Christ. In this sense, living a Christian life means simply appreciating God's sacrifice for the sake of our wholeness and welcoming his transformation of our lives. This conversion is continual.

Second, we can take at least five minutes for ourselves. This time might include a simple prayer of our willingness to "lean in," even though we're currently unable to see God's purposes for us on this particular day. We might ask God to give us a glimpse of his view of this day. Or we might take time to recall aspects of God's character that we know to be true or remember God's past activity in our lives. Through these exercises, we reaffirm our trust in his character and his activity, remembering that his work in our lives will not be in vain. Another way we might engage God's work in our lives is to enunciate three ways we presently feel God's work in us, noticing the ways he's changing us. We can observe similarities, differences, and correlations, noticing how his actions shape us for what we are currently encountering in life. Additionally, we might enunciate what God has impressed us to do and be throughout the course of our lives. We can remind ourselves that these goals, while not necessarily guaranteed to bear immediate fruit, are still worth striving toward because of the worthiness of the One who impressed them upon us. We can practice these things as we learn to take part in the eternal interaction between God and man, all the while keeping the grace God gives us before us.

Once, when visiting a large Baptist church in Texas, I heard a pastor give this invitation at the end of his sermon: "With all that you are and all that you know about Christ right now, will you respond?" This simple invitation is all John the Baptist responded to, and I believe it is the essence of what God asks of us each day. John dared to live into the reality of who God said he, in his true humanity, was. God asks us simply to do the same, to lean in toward our God-healed selves. We aren't Jane Austen characters; we won't see the full picture of our lives or know our full purposes ahead of time. But God asks us to live in response to all we know about who Christ is, and God asks us to let him change our lives accordingly. He asks us to notice that we cannot be fully human unless we realize humanity was made full already. May we know God, and may we truly know ourselves.

Learning the Art of Noticing

1. Take time to discover how God is reshaping your life. Think of three ways you can presently feel God's work in your life.
2. Ask God to give you a glimpse of his view of this day.

Note

1. Augustine, quoted in Thomas Merton, *Contemplative Prayer* (New York: Herder and Herder, 1969) 83.

Chapter 3

Noticing
God's Reality

God, our God, will take care of the hidden things, but the revealed things are our business. (Deuteronomy 29:29)

Christmas. There's something about the Advent season, a season named for the anticipation we feel. We enjoy the crisp, dry air that is somehow warmed by hospitality and love. We unpack wool sweaters, light our rooms with fireplaces, and spend evenings at home snuggling with family. Whether in solitude as we enjoy a warm bowl of potato soup or in a crowded auditorium as we listen to a child's Christmas concert, Advent urges us to celebrate "God with us." We make rich foods that comfort us, play music that inspires memories, and travel familiar roads toward family, all to honor the one who said, "Comfort ye, my people." It truly can be the most wonderful time of the year.

Except, one past Advent, while I lived in Texas, something was drastically wrong for me. The whole month before Christmas, it was 80 degrees. Though Muzak played in the stores and carolers still came to our front door, you could practically swim in the wet Texas air. Growing up in the Midwest spoiled me with the wonderful combination of cool weather and warm electric blankets. By that point, I'd lived in Texas for a while; I knew better than to expect snow. But that year, singing "Joy to the World" while wearing shorts and flip-flops was bitter for me. I made the same holiday preparations and read the same Advent Scriptures that I do each year, but try as I might, I could not jumpstart my soul into the season. I know people throughout the southern hemisphere have a warm holiday every year, but this past Christmas was not what I expected. Eighty-degree weather was not in my holiday plan.

What is it about our expectations, plans, or ideas that hold such sway over us? It is as if we've written a script for a play of our lives that runs about a month ahead of actual life; if reality varies from what we've created in our minds, we disengage or pout. Maybe the vacation home we rented for a week wasn't as we pictured it would be. The ringing phone interrupted the afternoon we planned. Another ad agent dominated a meeting we called by discussing a new project idea. Somehow, if our day hasn't gone according to plan, we face it reluctantly.

Author Denise Roy talks about our attachment to our own will, calling it *Plan A.* "My trouble," she says, "is that I think there is a track that things should stay on. I'm hooked to a belief that life *should* go a certain way. I develop an attachment to Plan A and set up my expectations accordingly. An important part of spiritual practice is to learn to let go, to recognize that Plan A exists only in my head."[1] We need to learn to dive into reality with all of our energies instead of reluctantly dipping our toes into life because it doesn't flow with our expectations.

We do this with our faith, too, don't we? We prize the way we understand and experience God as the only way to do so, which makes us slow to accept the experiences of others that differ from our own. We quickly forget that our view simply cannot be the full view of the Christian life. We church folk are good at elevating our expectations or experiences to unmovable cornerstones of faith. We struggle to let God be bigger than our understanding of him. I've noticed this difficulty not only within my Baptist tradition, which boldly waves the flag of autonomy of the local church; I've noticed it in myself. While there are certain threads that typically weave a kingdom of God pattern, we consistently need to remind ourselves that "there is no culture that is a totally adequate human expression or a single approach to the Kingdom of God."[2]

How we engage life and faith over and above our understanding of them makes a difference not only in our personal experience, but also in the faith experiences of others. How many conflicts are caused, both in matters of faith and in everyday life, simply because we want our Plan A to win out over someone else's? How do we damage the loving attitude we desire to portray when we don't bridge the gap between our desires and those of someone else? What is more, how do we limit our faith journeys in an effort to experience our personal faith Plan A instead of God's reality?

There is much we don't and won't know about God. We need to notice this truth and get comfortable with it. Theologians call this idea the "transcendence of God," which is another way of saying (1) we recognize that we are not God or even a god, and (2) we see that there is a big gap between

God and ourselves. Keeping these ideas before us is a good beginning to experiencing reality as it *is*, not as we think it *should be*. Theologian and author A. J. Conyers says we "must begin with the honest admission that the things of God are too high and wonderful for humans to know, for God is essentially incomprehensible" (see Ps 139:6).[3] This recognition is vital to learning the art of noticing, because it helps us respond in humility to who God is and what he is revealing. Conyers put it like this: "The immense distance between God and humanity is the indispensable backdrop to a Christian idea of revelation. To reduce God to the level of human thought and human imagination, so that we can comprehend God, is to lose a sense of the very thing that distinguishes God as God."[4] The Swiss theologian Karl Barth spoke of this concept as the "hiddenness of God." It reminds us that only by God's grace can we experience God in the first place. This hiddenness of God is our starting point, where we realize that we begin to know God only through God's efforts to reach out to us.

Many times this idea of a transcendent God gets a bad reputation. It shows up as the summation sentence in a difficult Sunday school lesson or the answer a pastor gives to a church member's "out of bounds" question. "Well, son," it usually goes, "we just need to trust that God's ways are not our ways and leave it at that." This statement is true, and the ending of the book of Job seems to agree. However, God is not a grump who slaps our hands away from the cookie jar of omniscience. God doesn't play transcendence like a trump card. Or maybe he does, but we're on *his* team when he plays it. We don't have to sigh away his transcendence with our unanswered questions and our unfulfilled expectations. We get to *embrace* the fact that God is far outside of anything we can conceive and that he accomplishes the spectacular. We should notice and celebrate the fact that God's plan is not our plan, because his plan trumps ours; it is "far more than you could ever imagine or guess or request in your wildest dreams," as Ephesians 3:20 says.

I've just read through Exodus and Deuteronomy, and I think that without a doubt, the Israelites are the biggest group of whiners in the Bible. Every time you pick up the Pentateuch, here they come to Moses, complaining about how bad their lives are and how good they had it back in Egypt, even though they were slaves at the time. "Why did God drag us out here in the desert just to kill us?" they cry. On and on until you want to shout aloud "*Hello!* You've just walked through the Red Sea on dry land. God is leading you with a cloud and with fire. He's giving you water, he's giving you manna, he's giving you quail! Your clothes and your shoes are not wearing out. He's defeated other nations before you. He's made you his people who will be a part of eternal history, and yet you want to go *back*?"

Of course, I can't yell that loudly, unless I do it in front of a mirror. The Israelites' problem was not only their problem; it is mine as well. The Israelites could not see God's reality and wanted to stick with their own version of life, even though it was a bad situation in the first place. They were so closed to God's transcendent ways, so unwilling to notice what God was doing around them, that they wanted to choose the sure, although bad, reality. They knew what to expect in Egypt; it was their Plan A, and they resented Moses and his Yahweh for presenting them with an unsure future. But what I know in hindsight—that God had amazing plans for this people beyond the scope of their understanding—is the same thing I forget as I live my life each day. I resent that my life doesn't follow my plan, when all the while I have this bewildering, transcendent God willing to reveal his reality to me. Why would I choose slavery over his promised land?

So many times, we Christians seem apologetic to nonbelievers that our faith lives are not scientifically explainable or quantifiable. The real question, to me, is why we would *want* to worship an explainable God. Shouldn't we celebrate the transcendent nature of God? Isn't this one of the reasons we believe—because God is so utterly other-than-human? If so, it would follow that, as believers, we would *want* God to do the unexpected, especially in our own lives. Eugene Peterson has said, "A solved life is a reduced life."[5] Why would we want our lives to be explainable by human means? Why would we want to follow our own earthly expectations?

If we take time to develop our noticing skills, we have the privilege of peeking into God's reality, for this world and for our lives. We have the opportunity to play the game of life on the side of the One holding the cards that will ultimately trump all. We need to daily dedicate ourselves to asking Jesus how he sees the world and then notice and respond to what he reveals. We can make our own plans and judge them by our narrow expectations, or we can experience life as the boundless reality of the One who created it. It's our choice, and while most would quickly, cognitively choose the latter, it takes daily awareness and action to live life according to God's reality or according to the way things truly, in their deepest sense, *are*. Thomas Merton believes that all the things we do in our lives as Christians, such as prayer, reading, meditation, and worship, are aimed at *purity of heart*. This is his term for what he calls "a new spiritual identity—the 'self' as recognized in the context of realities willed by God."[6] When we can free ourselves from our limited ideas and draw on Christ's word-made-flesh worldview, we open ourselves to life as it was meant to be lived. And, while life in God's reality is not a guarantee for all bliss and beauty, on the global or personal level, it is an assurance of truth, wholeness, and fulfillment that nothing else can offer in this life and beyond.

The way I see it, I whined myself through what was probably a perfectly wonderful Advent; but did I tell you that it snowed that following Easter? It did. In Hewitt, Texas, in April, during Holy Week, it *snowed.* God sent the unexpected: big, beautiful, white feathers whirling down from above. I had to think of Jesus' followers and their complete despair at the death of the One who embodied all their hopes. How could they possibly conceive of Sunday? And, yet, there it was, falling in white flakes all around them, calling them to run outside and dance in God's reality, his victory over death and darkness. Let me tell you, I didn't mind wearing layers to church over my Easter sundress. This time, I noticed God's reality—and I danced in it.

Learning the Art of Noticing

1. Do you have a Plan A that keeps playing in your head? Do you have a Faith Plan A? Ask God if this is the plan to which he wants you to hold.
2. Today, remind yourself that "a solved life is a reduced life."[7]

Notes

1. Denise Roy, *Momfulness* (San Francisco: Jossey-Bass, 2007) 59–60.

2. Stuart C. Bate, ed., *Responsibility in a Time of AIDS* (Pietermaritzburg, South Africa: St. Augustine College, 2003) 94.

3. A. J. Conyers, *A Basic Christian Theology* (Nashville: Broadman & Holman, 1995) 21.

4. Ibid.

5. Eugene H. Peterson, *The Contemplative Pastor: Returning to the Art of Spiritual Direction* (Grand Rapids: Eerdmans, 1989) 64.

6. Thomas Merton, *Contemplative Prayer* (New York: Herder and Herder, 1969) 68.

7. Peterson, *Contemplative Pastor*, 64.

Chapter 4

Noticing Immanuel

For me, the Incarnation is the place, if you will, where hope contends with fear. Not an antique doctrine at all, but reality—as ordinary as my everyday struggles with fears great and small, as exalted as the hope that allows me some measure of peace when I soldier on in the daily round.

—Kathleen Norris[1]

It was a fairly large room made of sloppily painted concrete block. The walls were the usual hospital off-white and were decorated with educational health posters and pictures of generic, serene images, like "Castles of Europe." There were probably forty wooden chairs in the room that had been dragged into multiple configurations over the years, and showed the wear. This day, we arranged them into an oval and tried to sit closely for warmth in the chilly building. Around twenty attendees slipped in and out of the meeting when their time to see the doctor came.

We began as usual, with our leader, Pauline, welcoming everyone, explaining what a support group was, and asking us all to use English if we could. The first few times I attended, I thought she said this for my benefit, being an American outsider in the room. Later, I found out that English was a leveler; it was not the white or the black language, but a "non-political" one that most could understand.

Usually it took people a while to open up and share with the group. Sometimes we talked about nutrition and our immune systems. Sometimes we talked about condoms and infection control. Sometimes we talked about stigma and the members' fear of disclosing their HIV positive status to spouses, parents, or boyfriends. But this day, a woman named Sarah jumped in first, with gusto.

It was the first time I'd seen her at the clinic or the support group. She was extremely tall, thin, and had short, stylish black hair. She was wearing makeup, a short black skirt, and black knee-high boots. I had to concentrate to understand what she was saying, for even though she was speaking English, her Swazi accent and the angry tone of her words rushed by me.

She told us her story in a staccato voice, so that even those who understood the Zulu she sprinkled in had to ask her to repeat herself. Her story was different from that of so many others, as she had already disclosed her HIV positive status to family and friends. This was not a small confession, though she found she was eventually accepted with compassion. However, her husband of several years had recently left her for another woman and taken their children with him. She was not allowed to see or speak to her son and daughter. She was not crying, but angry, and wanted to know how she could at least get her children back. Pauline suggested she could start by contacting the attorneys working with the AIDS Law Project, and she gave Sarah a phone number. Then Sarah went further. How could she make a living for herself, a woman without a job and without skills? How could she provide for her children—if she could ever get them back—on her own? She asked all the questions that a woman in such a dependent place in society asks, questions that we had heard discussed so many times over the past few months.

As she spoke, my mind began to catalog all the stories we had heard as we sat in that support group. There was the woman who, after disclosing her status to her mother, had been made to sleep in a bathtub in the family's concrete block home. There was the woman who had been turned out altogether by her husband of nine years, along with a child, and who asked the group for advice on where to live. There was the teenager whose boyfriend had taken her out to a fancy dinner just the week before, only to disclose to her his HIV positive status and to tell her that she was probably HIV positive also. There was the black man in AIDS stage who worsened week after week, brought to the clinic by an Afrikaans woman. There was the woman in her sixties who said, "I've been married for forty years, and I know *I've* been faithful." There was the mother considering an abortion, and another who asked us to take her infant with us to America so she, the mother, could have a better life.

My mind reeled as I sat in the support group that day. My role in the group was as a chaplain of sorts, to offer spiritual support when needed. Some days I offered comments on faith (that had to be translated). Other days, my role was simply to be a white person who cared about the suffering of her black peers. I was an outsider in almost every way, but I desired to show up and love, to be a white-faced American who cared. But that day, while listening to Sarah's story unfold, I only wanted to curl up into the fetal position in my chair. My body felt wrung out; I was overwhelmed by these lives in crises. Listening to woman after woman living in unimaginable desperation, I could not begin to understand the roads these women traveled home each time the support group broke for the day. I had sympathy, but was incapable of empathy. Their crises brought about my own. I felt, maybe for the first time in my life, *complete helplessness.* There was absolutely nothing I could do that day to help Sarah's situation. All the seminary training I could muster up, all the money or legal help I could obtain for her, all the words of faith I might share would not bring her children back or allow her to support herself well in a country with such ingrained systemic problems. I began to ache. As Madeleine L'Engle said in one of her books, "It hurts . . . that love is not enough."[2]

I decided to join a yoga class of older, Jewish women. I prayed a lot and read poetry. I had many long talks over hot cups of rooibos tea with my husband and with close friends. I joined a Bible study group with people who ran a foster home for AIDS orphans and thus faced similar obstacles. I spent time with Sarah. I received Communion during evening masses at an Anglican church that warmly welcomed this lifelong Baptist. I took long walks with my husband . . . long walks. And I listened to a lot of Dave Matthews.

My husband and I bought Dave's solo album, *Some Devil,* on a South African road trip one weekend. The shy, loving spirituality of the lyrics alongside his rhythmic arrangements refreshed us deep down. We loved it not only for the album's musicality, but because we knew that Dave was born in Johannesburg and moved back and forth between South Africa and the States as he grew up. It was comforting to listen to; we felt that Dave knew our issues. He knew our state of helplessness, our conflicted worldviews, and our sleepless nights. He held the place close, he loved its people, he knew its past. "South Africa," he once said, "gives me a perspective of what's real and what's not real. America's very far from a state of natural existence."[3] My blinders were off; I now knew what my female peers halfway around the world faced every day. Having Dave's voice alongside me comforted me in my helplessness. My husband and I brought scholarly books with us for our schoolwork that were supposed to help us think about "the issues" in context. These books all had titles like *Reading Karl Barth in South Africa* and *Reading Bonhoeffer in South Africa.* These books were well and good, but the editors who collected the essays did so in places like Grand Rapids, and that didn't really help me in Jo'burg. There were no easy answers here; Dave seemed to know that and sit alongside us anyway.

One of the most jarring realities we notice in a life of faith is that this is exactly what God does. He comes to sit beside us in our helplessness and belts out the lyrics our hearts are trying to make sense of. He did this through the historical person of Jesus Christ and does it today through the living person of Jesus Christ that is in each of his followers. The big word for this concept is Incarnation, but God simply told us to think of Jesus as Immanuel, which means "God with us." How amazing that one of the main ways God wants us to think about the person of Jesus is as "a sharing, an embrace of life by Life, a total identification of God with the object of his love."[4]

We see the idea that God journeys with us in Christ throughout the Bible. The writer of the Gospel of John begins his account with the idea that Jesus is the central theme of God's relationship to humans, that he is the one true Word, or *logos,* that God wishes to speak to us. John begins his account with this idea, wanting everything he writes afterward to be read through the lens of these two concepts: that "the Word was with God" (1:1, NIV) and that "the Word became flesh and made his dwelling among us" (1:14, NIV).

The idea of *making one's dwelling* is something that would have made bells go off in the minds of some of the first people to hear it. Immediately, the language John uses here would have connected first-century Jews with their old, old stories of the ways in which God journeyed with them in the past. It would have caused them to think about God's promise to dwell with his people in Ezekiel 37:27. This verb comes from the same root word as the noun for "tabernacle" or "tent," which is the place where "the LORD used to speak to Moses face to face, as one speaks to a friend" (Exod 33:9).[5] John is saying that God "now meets and journeys with the people in Jesus Christ."[6]

Jesus knows what it is like to be human, because, along with being "God with us," he was fully human. He humbled himself and identified with us in all the world's particularity, in *human* particularity. Athanasius wrote, "The incarnate Word moved among people, becoming an object of their senses, healing and touching by word and deed."[7] This is hard for us to understand, so much so that some of the earliest controversies in Christianity were not over people questioning Jesus' divinity, but his true humanity. Jesus' being everything that we are has been problematic then and now. Eugene Peterson writes,

> This has never been an easy truth for people to swallow. There are always plenty of people around who will have none of this particularity: human ordinariness, bodily fluids, raw emotions of anger and disgust, fatigue and loneliness. Birth is painful. Babies are inconvenient and messy. There is immense trouble in having children. God having a baby? It's far easier to accept God as the Creator of the majestic mountains, the rolling sea, the delicate wildflowers, fanciful unicorns, and "tygers, tygers burning bright" (to quote William Blake).[8]

What does it mean to us to know that Christ, who knows exactly what it is to be human, meets us, each along our own paths, and journeys with us? Take time to consider the following lyrics and be thankful for the One who is willing to make the trip of life with us:

What a friend we have in Jesus,
All our sins and griefs to bear!
What a privilege to carry
Everything to God in prayer!
Oh, what peace we often forfeit,
Oh, what needless pain we bear,
All because we do not carry
Everything to God in prayer.

Have we trials and temptations?
Is there trouble anywhere?
We should never be discouraged,
Take it to the Lord in prayer:
Can we find a friend so faithful
Who will all our sorrows share?
Jesus knows our ev'ry weakness,
Take it to the Lord in prayer.

Are we weak and heavy laden,
Cumbered with a load of care?

Precious Savior, still our refuge;
Take it to the Lord in prayer:
Do thy friends despise, forsake thee?
Take it to the Lord in prayer;
In his arms he'll take and shield thee;
Thou wilt find a solace there.[9]

We must be mindful of the Incarnation. *We have the privilege of "God with us" if we choose to notice and recognize it.* May we offer praise that God has chosen to identify himself with us through Jesus, making the effort to "meet the needs of his people and reveal God fully to humankind."[10]

There is more we need to notice, however, about God's desire to identify with us. As we've said before, "the story of Jesus is a way of talking about God."[11] Christ was fully human, but also fully divine, revealing God's character to us. The fact that God journeys with us is encouraging, but it also must be humbling. The doctrine of the incarnation is not just wish fulfillment on the part of humans. Jesus is not merely a buddy, not only our "homeboy," as read a shirt I once saw. We don't treat Jesus like a puppy, soaking in his excitement over our coming home and then leading him back to stay in the laundry room when we go out to begin another day. We must remember that it is through God's action and God's desire that he identifies with us through Jesus. It is a grace we may aspire to but one for which we dare not take credit.

The second chapter of Philippians helps remind us not to turn "God with us" into "Jesus is my best-friend-of-the-week." Verse 6 begins, in RSV,

> Though he was in the form of God, he did not regard equality with God as something to be exploited, but emptied himself, taking the form of a slave, being born in human likeness. And being found in human form, he humbled himself and became obedient to the point of death—even death on a cross. Therefore God also highly exalted him and gave him the name that is above every name, so that at the name of Jesus every knee should bend, in heaven and on earth and under the earth, and every tongue should confess that Jesus Christ is Lord, to the glory of God the Father.

Our understanding of Jesus and his willingness to come alongside us should always be tempered with the fact that he was willing to die for us. He not only identifies with us in our ultimate despair, but also sanctifies us and saves us from it. Consider the second part of Ezekiel 37:27-28, here in the NRSV:

"My dwelling place shall be with them; and I will be their God, and they shall be my people. *Then the nations shall know that I the LORD sanctify Israel, when my sanctuary is among them forevermore.*"[12] It is not just so that we can all feel happy and consoled that Jesus identifies with us in our humanity; it is so that he can cleanse us and gift us with a claim to his divinity. It is in our humility that Jesus is able to rescue us in time of need or to sustain us simply by occupying the chair next to us in a circle of women at an HIV clinic.

"Yesterday at support group," my journal from September 17, 2003, reads, "a mother needed to leave the room and she reached across a few chairs and gave me her child to hold while she left." In a culture of such communal mothering, I was so graced that she chose me, the outsider, to hold her child while she was in the next room seeing the doctor. Amid stinging despair, identification birthed a moment of hope and love. And this was Immanuel to me.

Learning the Art of Noticing

1. Voice a prayer of thanks for God's total identification with us, the objects of his love.
2. Enjoy the privilege of taking things to the Lord in prayer today, remembering that he's traveling with us.

Notes

1. Kathleen Norris, *Amazing Grace: A Vocabulary of Faith* (New York: Riverhead Books, 1998) 30.

2. Madeleine L'Engle, *The Summer of the Great-Grandmother* (Farrar, Straus & Giroux, 1974; repr., New York: HarperCollins) 32.

3. Dave Matthews, "My African Heart," *Time Magazine*, 15 September 2001.

4. Theodore G. Stylianopoulos, "Jesus Christ—the Life of the World," *Greek Orthodox Theological Review* 28/0017-38944 (Summer 1983): 139.

5. Ideas in this paragraph are from Gail R. O'Day, "John," *The New Interpreter's Bible: A Commentary in Twelve Volumes*, vol. 9 (Nashville: Abingdon Press, 1995) 522.

6. Charles Campbell, "John 1:1-14," *Interpretation* 49/4 (October 1995): 394, quoted by Matthew Sprink, "Flesh and Blood: The Incarnation and Its Impact on Missions," *The Truett Journal of Church and Mission* 1/1543-3552 (Spring 2003): 15.

7. Theodore G. Stylianopoulos, "Jesus Christ—the Life of the World," *Greek Orthodox Theological Review* 28 (Summer 1983): 139.

8. Eugene H. Peterson, *Christ Plays in the Thousand Places* (Grand Rapids: Eerdmans, 2005) 59.

9. Lyrics by Joseph Scriven (1855), *Baptist Hymnal* (Nashville: Convention Press, 1975) 403.

10. David J. MacLeod, "The incarnation of the Word: John 1:14," *Bibliotheca Sacra* 161/641 (Jan–Mar 2004): 73.

11. M. Eugene Boring, *The New Interpreter's Bible: A Commentary in Twelve Volumes* (Nashville: Abingdon Press, 1995) 8:138.

12. Italics mine.

Chapter 5

Noticing the Advocate

Bartender, please,
fill my glass for me
with the wine You gave Jesus that set him free
after three days in the ground.

—Dave Matthews[1]

"Have a good day." When you part from just about any person here in the United States, this is what you say or hear, isn't it? Whether we are ending a conversation with a cashier or lunch with a friend, it seems that our generic hope for all members of our society is that they "have a good day." This phrase, it seems, has almost become meaningless, a polite way to tie up a verbal interaction. Are we really trying to usher good into the lives of people we meet by saying, "Have a good day"? What do we mean by these words? If we could wish good into the days of others we meet, verbally or otherwise, what are we really wishing for them? What is a "good day"?

I wonder what Christians consider a good day. What makes me curious about this is a series of Bible studies I once attended where, regardless of the actual topic of focus each particular day, the recurring theme was how we as Christians fail to be "on fire for God." The theme went something like, "We don't spend our days focusing on God enough, and we fail to be the people we should be for God. We get distracted by our work, our kids, and our schedules. We forget to concentrate on God. We need to stay on fire for God." Ultimately, I believe the leader of the Bible study nobly attempted to push people beyond the doldrums of daily life to a place where they would live intentionally, following the example of Christ. What he communicated, however, was a sense of guilt for the way life's involvements seemed to confuse the way he lived out his faith.

My husband and I found this struggle evident as we worked with college students at Baylor. It was amazing to see young people begin to take hold of their own faith, deeply examining aspects of their beliefs that they once took for granted. They worked hard to match their career choices, their dating habits, and their priorities to their understanding of faith and what was "good." But what *was* "good"?

We'd often invite the students to play a little game with us, asking them, "If you were to have the ultimate day as a follower of Christ, what would that look like? Let's say our pastor, Brother Ron, was to give you a Brother Ron Cam for a day, letting him see video feed of everything you did. What in your daily life would reveal your faith to him? Would you try to go around quoting Bible verses to people all day instead of actually speaking to them? Would you stop humming that Aerosmith song and begin humming 'Shout to the Lord?'" Then, we would enjoy great discussions among the students about what Brother Ron's idea of a "good day" was, what the students' ideas were, and whether they were supposed to match up. Ultimately, the struggle to reconcile the power of our faith with our tasks, vocations, and relationships could be the biggest challenge we face as believers. We enjoy Sunday mornings, but what difference do they make in our lives on a Tuesday or a Thursday?

Is this guilty struggle to manage our "God stuff" and "life stuff" really what God envisions for his followers? How are we evaluating ourselves and by whose rubric? Are we suffering from some kind of spiritual anorexia, paralyzing ourselves with false guilt about how we're "not where we should be," spiritually speaking? Are we not able to rest until we think we've attained the "good Christian life"? Or do we put faith and life into separate compartments in our lives because it's easier if they don't mix? We've been called to hope in Christ, hope for a lifetime of "good days," but do we experience them?

What is life supposed to look like? What is *my life* supposed to look like? As Christ's followers, isn't that *really* what we want to know? These questions we ask are the same questions another group of Jesus' followers asked thousands of years ago. We can read this conversation in John 14, when Jesus tells his followers that he is about to leave them, that life for him and his followers won't always look like it does just now. What was going through their heads? "Okay, so all this stuff about love, about your kingdom. What difference is that going to make if you're going away? Was it all just flowery faith language? Because I have this life here. I've got this fishing business. How do

I go and pick my fishing nets back up now? How do I reconcile your love with my lures? What is my life supposed to look like?"

Jesus, anticipating our need to reconcile his love and our everyday lives, tells us about the Advocate he sends us. You might have heard this part of the Trinity referred to as the Holy Spirit or the Paraclete. However, before you conjure up images in your mind of a Little You that sits on your shoulder and tells you what you should or shouldn't do, listen to Jesus' description. He simply says we have an Advocate, a Friend, an Encourager. He calls him the Spirit of Truth that will be in us (vv. 16-17).

How does it make us feel that we have an Advocate? What difference does it make that we have a Holy Friend who wants us to experience life at its fullest? We have someone who is on our side, rooting for us to live into the work God does in our lives. Jesus didn't send us a Jesus Cam or a Holy Taboo Player to monitor us and buzz us in the face every time we say or do something we shouldn't. He sent us an Advocate, a Spirit of Truth, to remind us who we are to him and who he's consistently creating us to be.

Do we listen to that voice within us? Do we listen to the voice that is on our side, asking on our behalf, reminding us who we are re-created to be in Christ? Jesus says this voice will be our counselor and encourager when we struggle to reconcile Sunday with Tuesday. This Spirit refreshes us and breathes the power of God into our everyday experiences. Theologian A. J. Conyers explains the Spirit like this: "That which men and women had deeply and desperately longed for is made available to them—reconciliation with God in their everyday works, their profoundest desires, and their constant striving."[2]

Do we notice our Advocate? To what are we listening? We must give time to noticing the ideas that run through our minds, for often our thoughts determine our actions. When we go through our days, are we thinking about what happened years ago? Do we have thoughts of fear about what might happen tomorrow? Are we thinking, "Mom would've wanted it this way"? Or, are we engaged in what we say and do in the present? Jesus tells us the Spirit of Truth is in us and will guide us. He will tell us what a "good day" should look like. Noticing the thoughts that influence us moment by moment and then submitting them to the Spirit of Truth helps us begin to align our priorities and actions with those of God and his love.

In Romans 8:5-11, Paul helps us by contrasting a life characterized by moral striving with a life in which we attend to the Spirit of truth. He draws sharp distinctions between the two, so maybe this passage is best understood in a chart such as this:

	Living on Your Own	Living in the Spirit
8:5	Those who think they can do it on their own end up obsessed with measuring their own moral muscle but never get around to exercising it in real life.	Those who trust God's action in them find that God's Spirit is in them—living and breathing God!
8:6	Obsession with self in these matters is a dead end;	attention to God leads us out into the open, into a spacious, free life.
8:7	Focusing on the self is the opposite of focusing on God. Anyone completely absorbed in self ignores God, ends up thinking more about self than God. That person ignores who God is and what he is doing.	
8:8	And God isn't pleased with being ignored.	
8:9a		But if God himself has taken up residence in your life, you can hardly be thinking more of yourself than of him.
8:9b	Anyone, of course, who has not welcomed this invisible but clearly present God, the Spirit of Christ, won't know what we're talking about.	
8:10		But for you who welcome him, in whom he dwells—even though you still experience all the limitations of sin—you yourself experience life on God's terms.
8:11		It stands to reason, doesn't it, that if the alive-and-present God who raised Jesus from the dead moves into your life, he'll do the same thing in you that he did in Jesus, bringing you alive to himself? When God lives and breathes in you (and he does, as surely as he did in Jesus), you are delivered from that dead life. With his Spirit living in you, your body will be as alive as Christ's!

This, then, is our Helper, God living and breathing in us. Look at verse 10 again. It says this intentional effort to listen to the Spirit is the way to experience life on God's terms. This is how we begin to live the real, true, meaningful life that our Creator wants for us. It is how we "have a good day." We begin to understand that a "good day" is not just the absence of conflict or the presence of pleasant circumstances, but much more. It is more than avoiding the no-no's of life; it is a loud "Yes!" to what is important in this life. It is being able to live in the truth of how the world is and how we fit into it. In Galatians 5:22-23, Paul describes life in the Holy Spirit like this:

> He brings gifts into our lives, much the same way that fruit appears in an orchard—things like affection for others, exuberance about life, serenity. We develop a willingness to stick with things, a sense of compassion in the heart, and a conviction that a basic holiness permeates things and people. We find ourselves involved in loyal commitments, not needing to force our way in life, able to marshal and direct our energies wisely.

Who doesn't want life like that? It's a gift to us if we are willing to notice the Advocate and be obedient to live in love as he directs. It's up to us to pause, quiet ourselves in the midst of the frenzy of life, and take direction from the Holy Spirit.

Recently, I met a friend from high school who now has three children. As we caught up on each other's lives, I told her of our family's upcoming transition from one to two children, adding, "I'll take all the advice you've got!" She paused, looked at me, and said, "Breathe." And while we laughed about it then, her advice has been such a grace to my temporary frustrations and impatience as a mom. Pausing to take a long, deep breath helps in the midst of getting my daughter in the car seat or through the bath and bedtime routine. It helps me to pause and listen to the Spirit of Truth tell me what's really important at that moment.

It's no wonder that one of the Old Testament images for the Spirit is "breath." Author Denise Roy says taking a few deep, intentional breaths is a way of praying and receiving the grace that's been given to us. "When we link our breath to the power of Spirit . . . we open up a channel of healing and wholeness that is available to us in any moment."[3] I like to breathe in, thinking of the Genesis creation story where the Spirit of God hovers over the chaotic waters, creating beauty and order out of disarray.

While we gain a sense of presence and wholeness from the Spirit, we must notice that the Spirit is not merely a disembodied life coach that helps us feel good. Rather, he urges us to take specific action to add the goodness of Jesus to our lives, working out that lifestyle in community with other followers. It is "incumbent upon the faith community to engage in disciplined conversation between the story of Jesus and their own stories."[4] This is what living by the Spirit is: making sure that in each moment, the love and life of God transforms your own story. Paul says it like this in Galatians 5:25: "Since this is the kind of life we have chosen, the life of the Spirit, let us make sure that we do not just hold it as an idea in our heads or a sentiment in our hearts, but work out its implications in every detail of our lives."

The Holy Spirit can guide us through every detail of our days, and he's the perfect one to do so because he lovingly knows us each in our particularity. He knows our quirks and our scenarios, our joys and our issues. He knows the person at work that exhausts me, the way the neighbor's barking dog grates my nerves, and the sweater I always wear when I want to feel lovely. He knows the decisions, fears, and frustrations we each face. He knows us and he loves us. He wants us to pause and take note of his Truth in difficult moments. He wants to give us his image for our lives, and if we seek him for it, we will find it. These images will not all be the same because of his particularity and our peculiarity. The mystery is how the Spirit works in our own histories, in our own emotions, and in our own worldviews to transform our part of the world for his kingdom purposes. Father, Son, and Holy Spirit work together to give us specific directions about who we should be, if we only ask. The Holy Spirit helps us find a healthy image of self and gives us "operating instructions," as Anne Lamott says, for living it out.[5] If we listen and follow, we no longer have to worry that we're not "on fire for God" according to someone else's opinion. We must notice and respond to *his* version of "good," as he is, himself, the ultimate good.

May we, as believers, see the privilege in the outworking of this mystery. May we fervently ask the Spirit of Truth to reveal himself to us, to show us our lives according to his image and purpose, as he sees us. May we see the world in his reality, according to his perspective and truth.

Have a good day.

Learning the Art of Noticing

1. Are you obsessed with measuring your own moral muscle, or are you trusting God's action in your life? Notice the difference today.
2. Breathe. Pause. Listen to the Spirit in specific moments of your day.

Notes

1. Dave Matthews and Tim Reynolds, "Bartender," *Live at Radio City*, CD, Walnut Water, LLC., 2007.

2. A. J. Conyers, *A Basic Christian Theology* (Nashville: Broadman & Holman, 1995) 134.

3. Denise Roy, *Momfulness* (San Francisco: Jossey-Bass, 2007) 28–29.

4. Gail R. O'Day, "John" *The New Interpreter's Bible: A Commentary in Twelve Volumes*, vol. 9 (Nashville: Abingdon Press, 1995) 778.

5. Anne Lamott, *Operating Instructions: A Journal of My Son's First Year* (New York: Random House, 1993).

Chapter 6

Noticing When We Obstruct Christ

Love lives in sealed bottles of regret.

—Seán O'Faoláin[1]

I did something one weekend of which I am ashamed. I did something I can never take back and something for which I can never be sure of the ramifications.

It was a crisp Saturday morning in October, the kind when you want to sink under the covers in bed for a few extra minutes. That morning, however, we were up and at 'em because we had somewhere to be: the Baylor Homecoming parade. This was not your average parade; this parade, one we had attended each year for more than a decade, was touted as the largest and longest homecoming parade in the nation. Whatever had been said about it, for the little town of Waco, it was a big deal. Even if you had nothing to do with Baylor University the rest of the year, chances are, if you lived in Waco, you brought your kids out for a chance to catch Tootsie Rolls and get an early start on their Halloween sugar high. There were always many alumni as well from all over the country who returned to enjoy memories of their college days or show their kids where Mommy and Daddy met. Whatever the reason for attending it, the parade was quite an event in the little Central Texas town. I mean, who wouldn't enjoy an hour-long procession of cheerleaders, faculty, funny little cars driven by Shriners, small high school bands, and fraternity floats made of chicken wire and crepe paper? Envisioning such fun, we all got up early on a Saturday, bundled up our children, and waited expectantly along the parade route.

My husband and I had been going to the same spot to watch the parade for years. We hadn't let our secret out to many people, but our spot was right in front of the Bank of America on Austin Avenue. It was early in the parade route, so most of the people in the parade were still excited about waving to you (and they still had candy to throw). Some years, the bank even gave out free hot chocolate, donuts, and balloons. Matt and I had set up our rickety lawn chairs there since before we were married. Some years we would go with a bunch of friends, and sometimes we went on our own. I don't think we ever dreamed that we'd bring our daughter to the parade one day, but there we were one October, proud alums coming home with our little Baylor bear cub. Although I couldn't bring myself to put Lucy in one of those baby cheerleader outfits, I made sure she was properly dressed in her green and gold attire alongside her parents. (Never mind that you couldn't really see her school spirit under her coat.) We were ready for the parade to begin.

That's when it happened. A young family with three children came and stood right in front of our chairs, between us and the parade. It was a nice little family, and, from the look of their non-green and gold clothes, probably not alumni but a family from town coming out to enjoy the sights. *Great*, I thought. *We're not going to be able to see anything.* The three children had their plastic bags ready for candy gathering, and they showed no signs of moving down the route. The young mother turned around and met my eyes, and that's when I did the act of which I am so ashamed: I gave her a tight-lipped smile. This was not the kind of smile I had given to the other people around me that morning; it was a smile that said, "Your kids are in our way."

As soon as my face unformed, I was ashamed of what I had done. What a passive/aggressive thing to do, I reprimanded myself. As the parade started and candy began to fly through the air, I saw that my "smile" had its desired effect: the mother whispered something to the father, and the father called the children over to the side and out of our way. I didn't know if I should go apologize or forget it. After all, we could see the parade now. As gleaming band instruments and clowns went by, my horror at what I had done grew. What was more, the father, who was cheerful and smiley, kept offering candy he caught to *my* daughter. I tried to be extra friendly, to say, "Thanks so much, but she's too young to eat it," but, of course, I felt worse. He probably wasn't purposefully cloaking my sin, but I sure felt the rebuke. Wasn't I supposed to be a Christian? Wasn't I supposed to be the one who did good?

As float after float passed, I thought about my tight-lipped smile, and how it was the wrong thing to do on so many levels. What was my problem, anyway? Did I really think that three 3-foot-tall kids were blocking our view of the parade, complete with 20-foot floats and 75-foot-high balloon animals? And what was so wrong with them standing in front of my daughter?

At that age, she got excited just watching the ceiling fan go around and probably would have been tickled to watch the older kids catch candy. She didn't even know about parade candy yet, so she wouldn't have cared if she'd gone home without one piece. No, not even Lucy was an excuse for my behavior this time; the selfishness was all Mom's problem.

The fire engines interrupted my reverie, rounding up the end of the parade with a blast of their sirens that sent Lucy into a panic. When she was calm, I looked around and realized that the family next to us had left. We packed up our chairs and headed back to the Honda, having had a full morning.

You might be thinking, "Wow, Holly. I can't believe you were so unkind. I am putting your book down and will never again read anything you write." Or you might be saying, "Holly: Three words: Get. Over. It." If you are thinking the latter, don't let me off the hook so easily. I haven't quite let myself off yet. I *really noticed* my behavior that day. I noticed how it made me feel. I noticed how I think it made them feel. And I noticed that the master of divinity degree I have hanging on my wall didn't mean much when it came to mastering my own selfishness.

The lesson I learned that day was *not* that I wasn't perfect; I've known that and knew it then. I noticed how quickly a minute inconvenience brought out the worst in me. I noticed how, in an instant, one tiny action did tremendous injustice to who Christ is. How, you say? Well, I hardly needed to identify myself as a Christian before this family. I was dressed in green and gold, looking like an alumna of the largest Baptist university in the world. And, while Baylor University and Christianity are not always synonymous, in this part of the Bible Belt, this little family could easily assume that I was at least "religious." From the moment that tight-lipped smile left my lips, I damaged their idea of what someone who follows Christ is like. At that moment, I was an obstacle for this family's ability to understand who Christ is, if they didn't know him already. While cognitively I had devoted my life to uncovering Christ in our world, I had in actuality let a parade—no, my own interests—obscure him and damage his character.

Paul talks to the Corinthian Christ followers about this in the tenth chapter of the second letter he wrote to them. He is clarifying their purpose, advising them to employ the grace they've received from Christ for things like "smashing warped philosophies, tearing down barriers erected against the truth of God."[2] This first part of the passage is almost like a high school fight song or a rocking motivational anthem, isn't it? Yes, we Christians are all about smashing the world's warped philosophies in Christ's name! We long to tear down the barriers that prevent people from knowing the true Christ. For me, all of these big, societal issues come to mind: illiteracy, HIV/AIDS, the sex trade, lack of access to medical care and pharmaceuticals. Yes! We are to use the grace we receive in our relationship with Christ to share grace in the lives of others. Let's go! (I hear "The Eye of the Tiger" playing right now in the background.)

However, the thing I noticed that Saturday at the parade was that obstructions to Christ aren't just big issues like slavery and one-child policies in other countries. I noticed that obstructions are also selfish sins we don't master in our own lives, such as purposely unfriendly smiles. I noticed that my game-day play did not match the plays in the playbook I said I would follow. The next part of Paul's advice to the Corinthians says Christians should be "fitting every loose thought and emotion and impulse into the structure of life shaped by Christ." Had I remembered this on parade day, had I noticed my own selfish impulses and taken the time to sift them through Christ and his teachings, I could have kept those desires from obstructing this family's knowledge of who Christ is. Yes, our goal as Christians should be to do away with the things in *our world* that keep people from knowing the love and freedom of Christ. Equally, and maybe more so, our goal should be noticing and doing away with the things in our *own lives* that keep people from understanding Christ as well. After all, don't the systemic injustices usually grow from the individual ones?

If we take the time, we Christians will notice that the "warped philosophies" Paul was talking about still exist in our lives. If I look around my world, I notice that I still erect barriers against the truth of God, both willingly and unwillingly, in the quickest of moments. Praise be to God that the grace of Christ provides forgiveness for all, including us. He is the means and the motivation for sharing this hope and life with others. Christ's life in ours gives us the ability to rid our own lives of that which would obscure him. As Paul says, "Our tools are ready at hand for clearing the ground of every obstruction and building lives of obedience into maturity." May we be faithful to examine, tear down, and prepare the way of the Lord. May we be faithful to observe our own lives, be humble enough to admit our sins, and resilient enough to let God realign us toward his purposes.

Learning the Art of Noticing

1. At the end of the day, think back and notice whether any of the choices you made today obstructed Christ.

2. We can erect barriers against the truth of God in the quickest of moments. Think of a verse of Scripture or something that God has recently spoken to you that you can take with you today, bringing it to mind in those quickest of moments.

Notes

1. Seán O'Faoláin, "The Jungle of Love," *Saturday Evening Post*, 13 August 1966, in James B. Simpson, ed., *Simpson's Contemporary Quotations* (Boston: Houghton Mifflin Company, 1988) 4000, accessed at www.bartleby.com on 15 October 2008.

2. All Scripture in this chapter is from 2 Corinthians 10:2-5 in *The Message*.

Chapter 7

Noticing World Family

Don't think only about your own affairs, but be interested in others, too, and what they are doing. (Philippians 2:4, NLT)

One of the most memorable sporting events I've watched was a football game I saw on television a couple of years ago: January, NFL playoffs, Seattle at Green Bay. I didn't particularly care who won the game, although Brett Favre led Green Bay to a great victory. What was notable about the game to me was the weather and the fans who braved it. About midway through the first quarter, big, white flakes started to fall, so much so that by half time, Favre was able to scoop up a snowball to toss at a teammate. Even for Green Bay, this was a cold, wet contest. Field personnel swept large brooms over every ten-yard line marker so the players could remember where they were on the field. Snow mixed with mud, and when the players knelt down, their breath made vapor clouds up and down the line of scrimmage. The heavy snow made the ball hard to see on the television screen; I can't imagine what it was like to play with the swirling flakes hitting you in the face.

But then the cameras scanned Lambeau Field and Stadium, packed with 60,000 fans. They wore cheese heads, body paint, and all manner of green and gold glittery objects. Yes, they were soaked to the bone, but they still hoisted droopy signs that said, "Brett, Never Leave Us!" I'm not sure how many layers of clothing and blankets they wore (the commentator said he was wearing six layers), but if the people in Green Bay were cold, it had to be bitter out there.

Of course, the game was televised. The people in the stadium could have watched it from their recliners at home, covered in warm blankets, with bags of Cheetos in hand. It would've been much more comfortable and much,

much cheaper. But this was Green Bay. This was possibly Favre's last season. This was the *playoffs*. I was impressed, watching the game from *my* living room, by what the fans went through to be able to say three little words: "I was there."

To me, this type of dedication is what it means to be a global citizen. In a much broader sense than football, being a global citizen means showing up for the important struggles, pledging yourself toward what is right. It is sacrificing in order to have the privilege of being eyewitnesses to the way God works in the world. It is wearing things you might not normally wear. It is experiencing temperatures you don't normally prefer. It is being happy to cheer for those on your team during a blizzard and take it all in because, at any moment, history could be made. It is being inconvenienced but anticipating the miraculous. Global citizenship is not about bragging rights or about proving who is the most loyal; instead, it is about being willing to be one in a crowd of thousands joined by their common love.

Global citizenship means simply being willing to focus on the game, to notice the world and the people in it. It does not mean noticing *your* world, but *the* world. It means being conscious of the fact that you, and your country, are not the center of God's universe. It is the recognition that the world is made up of people with similar needs, desires, responsibilities, and dreams. It is the willingness to connect to people all over the world, realizing that the choices you make each day affect them and that their decisions affect you. It is noticing that the world is your family.

Being a global citizen also means you must observe on a spiritual level, noticing the ways God works in our world. Global citizenship stems from a joyful, active curiosity that longs to know what God's kingdom looks like as it comes and changes countries and cultures all over the world. Just as we notice change in ourselves, we have the opportunity to witness how Jesus Christ changes people, makes communities whole, and redefines centuries-old societal norms. When God's activity breaks in, it is something we could never have planned ourselves, but something we can only plead for God himself to do. Noticing the world family is the ability to witness Jesus Christ and the change he brings both in our own lives and in the lives of others the world over. Jesus' last words were about this type of noticing: "And when the Holy Spirit comes on you, you will be able to be my witnesses in Jerusalem, all over Judea and Samaria, even to the ends of the world."[1]

This concept of being a witness, especially as we see it defined in the book of Luke, is not merely a passive awareness or a receiving of knowledge, nor is it a task we must perform door to door. Rather, it is a progression that takes place in our lives, as scholar Alan Culpepper describes in his commentary: "The concept of 'witness' develops in the course of the NT writings from the role of an eyewitness, to one who can testify to the gospel, to one who dies for the sake of the gospel."[2] We move from casual observer to one who can testify to the way our observations have affected our lives. As we continue to observe, our observations and their implications reinforce the truth of who we are and who God has re-created us to be, so much so that we would stake our lives on it. As witnesses of God's work in the world, we take note of the significance of Jesus Christ—both for our lives and for the lives of others—and then hungrily await the change it will bring to all of us.

Once we embrace the idea of what world family *is*, we tend to jump quickly to what we can *do*. While intentions are meaningless without action, activity minus careful thought soon proves shallow. Moving forward in this balance of being a witness, there are things we can do to give ourselves a spot on the fifty-yard line of the work God is doing in the world. There are faith postures we can practice to help us notice and engage the world.

First, *we must embrace the people of the world as family*, recognizing our common humanity. "The problem with the world," said Mother Teresa, "is that we draw the circle of our family too small."[3] Compassion doesn't rise from the belief that the evil in the world is somebody else's fault or that it is the result of poor choices a suffering person has made. Compassion arises from what Henri Nouwen calls a "constant willingness to see one's own pain and suffering as rising from the depth of the human condition that all men share."[4]

When I think of this communal mindset of family, I think of the times I sat in a circle of chatting South African women while children played around us. Anytime the conversation was interrupted by the shriek of a child who had fallen or needed attention, the woman closest to the shrieking child picked up the child and gave comfort, even if she was not the child's mother. We need to adopt this communal, compassionate worldview; when Christ reorients our understanding of love, anyone who needs comfort is called "family."

Second, *we must actively develop our global awareness*. We Americans are particularly unaware of the world around us at a time when such ignorance is costly, both to our culture and to our faith. Just watch *World News Tonight* and see how much of it is about our own country. Compare our news reports with those of other countries and you'll see that (1) people in other countries are much more educated and aware about global events, and (2) Americans seem to insulate themselves from the issues people around the globe are facing.

How did this happen? How did our melting pot/salad bowl land of opportunity become a nation of people who only shrug their shoulders at geography or struggles other humans face? We could blame the media and cry that our news is mainly entertainment. We could talk about how hard it is here in Small Town, U.S.A., to connect with people so far away (although with planes, the Internet, and e-mail, we really can't use that tactic anymore). We could make excuses about how we can't understand the complexity of the world and its problems, even as we hang diploma after diploma on our walls. Really, though, it's not about how others are not doing their job of educating us. It's not that the world is too far away or that we're not smart enough to begin understanding it. It's not that we *can't*; it's that we *don't*. We *choose* not to engage the world or learn of peoples different from ourselves.

We are a myopic culture. Maybe it's part of the American Dream philosophy bred in us from birth; Self-made Sallys and By-my-own-bootstraps Bills are some of the most honored people around. While the opportunity to improve yourself and your situation is a great thing, our striving to build perfect lives seems to have morphed into a perfectionism so focused on itself that we forget about others in the world. We work so hard to build the ultimate luxury sedan, to embody society's standard of beauty, and to achieve historical scientific breakthroughs that we conveniently forget our family members in other parts of the world who must walk miles each day in their only set of clothing for the opportunity to go to school.

How does this function on the Christian level? Are we working diligently to perfect our individual faith, while others live without the basics of the spiritual life? Are we attending three Bible studies a week, unaware that people in our own cities go without three square meals a day? If we allow our American mindset of consumption to spill into our understanding of what a Christian is, we are in danger of living irrespective of world family.

I know this danger because I lived it until the day of my twenty-fifth birthday. Birthdays still hold charm for me, but in October 2001, I was trying to keep the charm of my birthday alive. It was a long day of seminary courses, work in a local elementary school cafeteria, and then straight back to the seminary for a three-hour night course. My husband and I had agreed to have a late dinner together at my favorite Mexican restaurant, but first, I had to sit through a required missions class.

"Please take out a pen or pencil and prepare yourselves for a little quiz," said the professor as we settled into our seats. This was unexpected—so unexpected that I had let the charm of my birthday convince me that it was all right to leave some of the assigned reading undone. I remember nervously whispering to a friend next to me that I hadn't finished the assignments.

This quiz, however, had a different effect on me than I anticipated. I braced myself for a few minutes of panic-stricken answering, followed by a guilt-ridden hour or two in which I thought about how that quiz would affect my grade. I received a completely different experience. This quiz, which would not affect my grade, was given to assess my understanding of the world around me. During the next thirty minutes, I puzzled over a map on which we were to locate important world cities, as well as questions about birth rates, death rates, poverty, and gross national incomes. For some reason probably related to my own silliness, all my years of missions education in a Southern Baptist church (not to mention my high school and university degrees) had not prepared me to answer how many ethno-linguistic groups exist in the world or how many people in Sub-Saharan Africa are infected with HIV.

As we spent the next three hours going over the answers of the quiz together, I was continually stunned, not only by the state of our world and the lives of the people in it, but by my complete ignorance of it all. I was ashamed that I had only memorized facts and figures before, and devised cute acronyms (which I quickly forgot after the exams) to help me memorize the world map. I had not recognized the life that existed in the world, lives of people whom God created. Outside of my effort to obtain good grades in geography or merits in church programs, I had not cared about what was happening in the world.

Until then, I believe my theology must not have *really* held that the life of Jesus Christ had any effect on what was happening in the world. I knew about poverty, ecology, politics, and economics, but those seemed like separate files in a drawer labeled "Real World." The other drawer, call it "Faith in Jesus Christ," held church words and phrases, experiences at camp, and stories of how my personal life had intersected with the gospel. That seminary class on my birthday set me out on the journey of reorganization. At the bottom of my notes from that evening, I scrawled, "What does this all mean for Christianity?" and "What does this mean for me?"

It seems I encountered the micro/macro issue. I knew that the gospel was applicable to individuals—to myself, my friends, etc. I knew that a life lived in relationship with Jesus Christ made a difference in who I was and what I was to be about. *But what I hadn't realized was that I was to be about the world.* Ironically, the girl from the Midwest who had petitioned out of her geography and world history courses in college ("I just *like* American history better.") was now struck with her own apathy for the world. I had not truly believed that Christ would affect the world and its people. Or, if I had believed it, I hadn't truly *cared for* that world.

I listened, awakened for the first time, as we discussed global trends such as tribalization and urbanization. I heard that in the year 2000, more than 300 cities in the world had a million people or more. I heard that more than 20 percent of the world's total population had no reliable access to food and water. I heard the statistics, but after that night, the statistics became real people. I later used my birthday money to buy an atlas so big it barely fit on our living room coffee table. I couldn't get enough of world news, current events, and the implications of each. I was being reorganized. My journey continued as I had the opportunity to study abroad the next summer in six different countries. Through this time, I learned I needed to quit trying to superimpose answers and instead humbly seek to discover what the global questions were. I needed to learn about and love my world family.

Virginia Woolf once wrote, "One of the signs of passing youth is the birth of a sense of fellowship with other human beings as we take our place among them."[5] It was my birthday, in many ways.

Seven years later, I sit typing in my home in Blue Springs, Missouri, the small suburb in which I grew up. I probably began my day in a manner similar to yours. I took a warm shower to begin my morning routine. I had milk and cereal to give my daughter when she woke up. I had a "to do" list waiting for me, complete with a gas-filled car in the garage to use to accomplish my tasks. I think of what Ralph Waldo Emerson wrote: "Though we travel the world over to find the beautiful, we must carry it with us or we find it not."[6]

We, as Christ-followers, find that *we must carry our observations with us.* Claiming membership in God's family requires us to live out of our global understanding, making choices that keep other people—both near and far—in mind. We must make decisions as if they affect those we've not even met because we now realize they do. We must live respective of world family.

If we take the state of our world to heart, this practice quickly gets tough. We feel guilt each time we turn on the water faucet when we know others don't have such access. We hush our whining about the high price of gas, remembering that most people don't have a car per person per household. We take home leftovers from a restaurant meal that could've fed four people, only to let them spoil in our huge refrigerators. It's easy to get overwhelmed, and many times we push all the thoughts in our heads aside, opting for our comfortable, real lives here because the truth is demanding. How is it that we don't become overwhelmed with guilt but still live as lovingly aware Christ-followers?

We begin by pushing through the difficulty, by paying attention to what is going on around the world, even though it is hard. Simone Weil, in her book *Waiting for God*, writes, "The capacity to give one's attention to a sufferer is a very rare and difficult thing; it is almost a miracle; it *is* a miracle."[7] We then place ourselves alongside others in the world. Elie Wiesel, Auschwitz concentration camp survivor and winner of the 1986 Nobel Peace Prize, urges us to become "a community in which all members will define themselves not by their own identity but by that of others."[8] This thought echoes Philippians 2:3-4: "In humility regard others as better than yourselves. Let each of you look not to your own interests, but to the interests of others" (NRSV).

What does this mean? It means I'm not defined by a trendy haircut or the labels on my clothes. It means I don't need to seek a house worthy of HGTV because that's not what defines me. It means that as long as there is suffering in the world, I must take responsibility for it because I am human. It means I have a part in the circumstances in our world right now, whether for good or for evil. Tennyson said, "I am a part of all that I have met."[9] My question is: am I playing a part for good or for evil in the lives of others around the world?

We must take responsibility for the evil that is and work toward the good, whether within our immediate neighborhoods or in a completely different hemisphere. I remember one time, during a visit with my family, someone brought up a story that had been on the news about a horrible crime committed upon a child in a nearby town. When each one of us, myself included, shook our heads, grew quiet, and sighed, my grandmother said, "Yes, we've gotten really bad, haven't we?" Her use of first person pronouns struck me. Here was my grandmother, a minister's wife and widow, verbally including herself with this criminal. But looking to the interests of others, as it says in Philippians 2, means that's what we're supposed to do. If suffering still exists, we're to take it upon ourselves, as the rest of

Philippians 2 says Christ did. We're to take responsibility for the evil that is and be willing to work for the good that is to come.

We're to dream big, the Bible says. For in the midst of suffering, exile, and the most overwhelming circumstances, the prophet Isaiah proclaims, to the nation of Israel and to us, that God is with us. Dream big of the good that is to come, he says, and work for it. Prepare for it, he says in chapter 54: "Sing, barren woman, who has never had a baby. Fill the air with song, you who've never experienced childbirth! You're ending up with far more children than all those childbearing women." God says so! "Clear lots of ground for your tents! Make your tents large. Spread out! Think big! Use plenty of rope, drive the tent pegs deep. You're going to need lots of elbow room for your growing family. . . . Don't be afraid—you're not going to be embarrassed."

We must work for the good and commit ourselves to postures of global selflessness, even if we can't figure out all the details surrounding the foreign dictators, food shortages, and fair trade. We're called to lean in, to work as hard as we can toward the good, and then trust in the God who says, "The way I work surpasses the way you work, and the way I think is beyond the way you think."[10] We're called to be witnesses of how God is at play in the world.

Sometimes, when we commit ourselves to global attentiveness, when we're willing to stand up on the sidelines through the blizzard, hoisting our rally signs and crying out for what is good, miracles happen. Sometimes the cries of those joining together from the stands muffle the play calls of the opposition. And the miracle isn't only the victory that occurs on the field. The miracle is that God's victorious grace chooses to include those who haven't worked out all season, those who can't withstand the big tackles, and those who don't have million-dollar contracts. The mystery is that by our willingness to observe and actively pledge ourselves to the good, he graciously and lovingly calls us not spectators, but contributors.

Learning the Art of Noticing
1. Each time as you watch the news, ask yourself, "How would the presence of Jesus change this situation?" Pray, talking and listening to God, about the news stories you hear.
2. Read one story about a country other than your own online or in a newspaper every day for a week.

Notes

1. Acts 1:8-9.

2. R. Alan Culpepper, "Luke" *The New Interpreter's Bible: A Commentary in Twelve Volumes*, vol. 9 (Nashville: Abingdon Press, 1995) 488.

3. Mother Teresa, quoted in Denise Roy, *Momfulness* (San Francisco: Jossey-Bass, 2007) 201.

4. Henri Nouwen, *The Wounded Healer* (New York: Doubleday, 1979) 88.

5. Virginia Woolf, "Hours in a Library," first published in "[The London] *Times* Literary Supplement" (30 November 1916); Robert Andrews, ed., *The Columbia Dictionary of Quotations* (New York: Columbia University Press, 1993) 16.

6. Ralph Waldo Emerson, "Art," *Essays, First Series* (1841, repr. 1847), http://www.emersoncentral.com/art.htm (accessed 14 September 2009).

7. Simone Weil, *Waiting for God* (New York: Harper & Row, 1973) 114.

8. Elie Wiesel, Afterword, in *Community of the Future*, Frances Hesselbein, Marshall Goldsmith, Richard Beckhard, Richard F. Schubert, eds. (SanFrancisco: Jossey-Bass, 1997) 273.

9. Alfred, Lord Tennyson, "Ulysses," in *Victorian Prose and Poetry*, ed. Lionel Trilling and Harold Bloom (New York: Oxford University Press, 1973) 416–18.

10. Within Isaiah 55:8-11.

Part II

Realignment

Introduction

The kingdom of this world is become the kingdom of our Lord and of his Christ, and he shall reign forever and ever. (Revelation 11:15)[1]

Once during a yoga class, my teacher announced that we would now venture into the exciting world of full arm balances, or handstands, as I knew them. After effortlessly demonstrating the posture against a wall, the instructor went person by person, helping each one in the class slowly kick up to the inversion briefly and then come back down again. I don't remember how I got up or how long I stayed up or even how it felt. I only remember Carole's words to me as she tried to get me to do something specific with my shoulders. I don't fully remember what I was supposed to do differently, only that while I was upside down, she tried two or three times to get me to adjust my shoulders. I somehow couldn't manage it. It wasn't that I didn't understand what she was asking me to do. It was that my shoulders simply wouldn't—or couldn't—do it. Then she said to me, matter-of-factly, "You just haven't developed that awareness yet. But it will come." Class after class, she tried different ways to communicate this awareness to me so that eventually I understood how I was meant to be aligned.

We see throughout the Bible that Jesus spent his life helping people develop their awareness of God and his kingdom, as the Gospels call it. Luke 8:1 says, "He went on through cities and villages, proclaiming and bringing the good news of the kingdom of God" (NRSV). Jesus was not proclaiming a system of feudal lords and medieval maidens. Rather, he simply spoke to people about God wherever he was and demonstrated the ways God was working in the world to bring all things into rightness. That state of wholeness, that proper alignment, is what Jesus called the kingdom of God. Before he ever died or rose again, Jesus worked to help people understand God's kingdom. Over and over, Jesus said, "What is the kingdom of God like? And to what should I compare it?"[2] He was trying to communicate this magnificent rightness on a level we could understand. Every metaphor, every parable, was a new way Jesus described how God is consistently at work to set things right. Jesus so wanted people to understand this that he sent out his disciples, who were developing this awareness of God, to speak about the kingdom and help bring healing and rightness (Luke 9:1). Even after bringing the ultimate rightness through his sacrificial death, Jesus appeared to them and still spoke to them about God's kingdom (Acts 1:3). We see here in the Bible that it wasn't really Jesus' goal to lead the coolest new Jewish sect or develop a religious system. Instead, he was about helping us develop our awareness of God and his good desires for our lives.

We see in Scripture that *following Jesus is not about us and what we're doing (or not doing); it's about noticing how God is making things right and then responding to that.* As we develop this art of noticing, we realize that it's not about spiraling inward on ourselves. Rather, Jesus was helping us to recognize the kingdom of God breaking in, to see how we're meant to be aligned. The book of Romans can help us here. Romans 3:10 says, "There's nobody living right, not even one, nobody who knows the score, nobody alert for God." Verse 6 of the same chapter asks, "How else would things ever get straightened out if God didn't do the straightening?" Verse 24 answers that question: "God did it for us. Out of sheer generosity he put us in right standing with himself. A pure gift. He got us out of the mess we're in and restored us to where he always wanted us to be. And he did it by means of Jesus Christ." Later, verse 27 sums up, "What we've learned is this: God does not respond to what we do; we respond to what God does."

Our realignment, we discover, means that we expectantly live into the rightness that God is working in the world; we let him work that rightness in us, adjusting and transforming us to be living examples of his wholeness. "Can you imagine," says Romans 5:17, "the breathtaking recovery life makes, sovereign life, in those who grasp with both hands this wildly extravagant life-gift, this grand setting-everything-right, that the one man Jesus Christ provides?" As Jesus adjusts us, we practice postures of faith, not striving to attain rightness on our own, but to confirm that God's rightness has come to us and is continually coming to the world (Rom 3:31). When we develop this kingdom awareness, we find that we don't struggle to do good for God. Rather, we become aware of the changes God makes to bring about his goodness in us. If we lean into God's realigning work in our lives, we discover that our maladies are cured and his health comes quickly. "But sin didn't, and doesn't, have a chance in competition with the aggressive forgiveness we call grace," says Romans 5:20-21. "When it's sin versus grace, grace wins hands down. All sin can do is threaten us with death, and that's the end of it. Grace, because God is putting everything together again through the Messiah, invites us into life—a life that goes on and on and on, world without end."

Jesus also asks us to adjust our thinking and move from a focus on the individual to an awareness of the communal. We also see from Scripture that *following Jesus is not just about personal holiness or individual change; it's about participating in God's setting-things-right worldwide.* Romans 3:25 says, "God sacrificed Jesus on the altar of *the world* to clear *that world* of sin. Having faith in him sets us in the clear. God decided on this course of action *in full view of the public*—to set *the world* in the clear with himself through the sacrifice of Jesus" (italics mine). Realignment, according to this verse, is not only for the individual; it is also a corporate reality that we seek.

According to what Paul writes here, awareness of self for the sake of ourselves is not where we stop; we employ what we gain from our awareness of ourselves and the world around us in order to bring about kingdom. "Obsession with self in these matters is a dead end," Paul says in Romans 8:6-7. "Attention to God leads us out into the open, into a spacious, free life. Focusing on the self is the opposite of focusing on God. Anyone absorbed in self ignores God, ends up thinking more about self than God. That person ignores who God is and what he is doing." We practice mindfulness in order to effect change, not only in ourselves, but also in the world. David Bosch writes, "To meet Christ means to become caught up in a mission to the world."[3]

This is important because it frames our idea of being a "good Christian." Jesus and Paul were trying to tell us that the kingdom of God means more than lots of self-control and several group Bible studies a week. Nineteenth-century German pietist Christoph Blumhardt recognized this. He preached once, "O yes, dear Christian, act in a way so that you die blessed. But the Lord Jesus wants more. He does not want my or your salvation, but the salvation of the whole world."[4] Blumhardt got it: the kingdom of God is not about individual piety but about the salvation of the world, individuals included. "It belongs to the greatest things we can say about Jesus," he said, "that he is not only concerned with the inside of humans, but that he also has a wide horizon of promise of life for the entire world. The life of human beings shall rise up by struggling for truth and peace in all respects."[5]

This knowledge should change the way we practice our faith. Our lives as Christ-followers are not merely day-to-day assessments of how we line up to Jesus' example. We don't do service projects to get merit badges. We lean into God's work in our lives to bring about changes that will align us—as individuals and as the wider world—to his kingdom values. This means if we have what we think is a "super-holy" life but don't work to bring rightness to the world, we miss the point. It's not only about individual alignment but about the wholeness of the world. I like the way Rob Bell put it once in an interview: "If Jesus comes to town and things don't get better, then we have to ask some hard questions."[6]

There is a difference between the type of Christianity that centers on the individual and the type of Christ-following that desires healing of the whole world. Blumhardt united his inward awareness of faith with his outward understanding of the world around him. "He saw the one in the other," says theologian Jürgen Moltmann of Blumhardt. "As we say today, think globally—act locally! He viewed the most intimate personal details in the light of the coming Kingdom and he saw the dawning Kingdom in the small matters of everyday life. And, most importantly, there was not religious mediation in between. The small personal life and the great arch of the Kingdom of God confronted each other in unmediated fashion."[7] God calls us to move "from religion to God's Kingdom, from the church to the world, from the concern for one's own person to the hope for the whole."[8]

When we begin to be realigned to the kingdom of God, we also notice that *the Christian faith is not only an inner, spiritual reality. Following Jesus is an active process that has outward political, social, and economic ramifications.* "Rebirth is not a private, inward event only," says Walter Wink, "for it also includes the necessity of dying to whatever in our social surroundings has shaped us inauthentically."[9] We are called to confront injustices in our day just as Christ confronted them, and was crucified for them, in his.

New Testament scholar Chris Marshall has a lot to say about this: "It is a drastic impoverishment of Jesus' message and a blunting of its radical edge to suggest that Jesus was only concerned with the spiritual needs and personal conduct of individuals."[10] He finds in Scripture that Jesus had a dual approach in helping us understand how to engage the injustices of the world. He denounced injustices and social evils and at the same time called together an alternative group of people to live out the values of the kingdom of God he proclaimed. This helps us know our role, not only as individuals, but as a community of Christians. Marshall says,

> The church as the community of the kingdom is called to a twofold political task. On the one hand, it is to proclaim the breakthrough of God's new order by giving visible expression in its own life to the peace, justice and righteousness of God's kingdom. On the other hand, it is to work tirelessly for peace and justice in surrounding society, to struggle against the forces

of the old age—forces of nationalism, militarism, materialism, sexism, and racism—which Christ has dethroned and which one day shall finally yield to God's glorious future.[11]

We must work toward the integration of faith and life, emerging out of Christian quietism into subversive kingdom work. We must notice and seek kingdom in our day-to-day activities; we must speak out against injustices. We must practice kingdom postures as we work toward God's wholeness enveloping the world. Paul writes to the Romans in 12:1-2,

> So here's what I want you to do, God helping you: Take your everyday, ordinary life—your sleeping, eating, going-to-work, and walking-around life—and place it before God as an offering . . . . Don't become so well-adjusted to your culture that you fit into it without even thinking. Instead, fix your attention on God. You'll be changed from the inside out. Readily recognize what he wants from you, and quickly respond to it.

As we continue to allow God to realign us toward his kingdom, we realize *Christianity is not just a hope for heaven someday.* We don't practice a faith of escapism, but we practice kingdom postures in hope that God's rightness is coming about and will continue to come about. Romans 3:26 says, "This is not only clear, but it's now—this is current history! God sets things right. He also makes it possible for us to live in his rightness."

This is important because it affects the way we act and speak about our faith. It changes the way we talk about our faith with others and what we view as the goal of our faith. If our faith is only about getting to heaven or staying out of hell, we're missing much of the wonder and joy that this life in Christ is about. If we do good deeds only for the sake of our own piety, we miss the ultimate goal of global wholeness God desires. Following Jesus *is* about the future, but not to the neglect of the present. It is about a faith life that is already changed and at the same time not yet fully realized. The kingdom of God *is* about eternity, and it is also about today. It is important for us to recognize this on an individual level, but also to communicate this to others. Our faith is about *so much more* than pursuing paradise; it is about pursuing Jesus and the kingdom that is making things right on the earth until global wholeness comes about in him someday. Jesus helps shape our understanding of this with his words to the Pharisees that are recorded in Luke 17:20-21. They wanted to know when the kingdom of God was coming, and he answered, "The kingdom of God doesn't come by counting the days on the calendar. Nor when someone says, 'Look here!' or, 'There it is!' And why? Because God's kingdom is already among you." James L. Boyce writes, "For disciples the promise of the kingdom is not a matter of control or security but of the persuasive power of a message and a person—the message of the good news about the one who calls, the one who goes to suffering and death and resurrection, the one who then calls all who wait on his return to live in watchful confidence that in him the kingdom has already come to us (13:32-37)."[12]

So what does all this mean? What are we ultimately to be about? First, *we must be able to notice the kingdom of God.* Ultimately, this is our goal in developing our awareness. We must be alert, noticing and proclaiming the ways God's kingdom is arriving in our world right now. We should be able to see the evidence of it in our day-to-day lives and to see the difference it makes in the world around us, just as Jesus did. He was always using new descriptions, voicing every possible metaphor to help us understand. I once read of a minister who was preaching through the passages where Jesus said, "The kingdom of God is like . . . ." He handed out paper with that heading on it and asked his congregation for new, personal expressions of the kingdom of God according to how each person had experienced it. If you received that paper and pen, what would you write? Are you aware of the ways that God and the wholeness he brings have rewritten your life and your world? Do you notice the re-creation of yourself and others? Where on the globe can you see God setting things right?

Second, *we must allow Christ to realign us, to help us practice in hope the postures of our faith that point toward ultimate wholeness.* We take up residence in this kingdom by letting him redirect our postures, or attitudes, toward life and health in him. We practice these postures as a visible sign of God's kingdom here on earth, working toward the kingdom coming to all parts and problems in the world. We practice in hope, not only that we will experience life now but also so that we, and the whole world, will someday be enveloped in the future God intends for all of us. Come, Lord Jesus.

Notes

1. Revelation 11:15, and the lyrics from the "Hallelujah Chorus" of Handel's *Messiah*.

2. Luke 13:18.

3. David J. Bosch, "Witness to the World," in *Perspectives on the World Christian Movement*, 3rd ed. (ed. Ralph D. Winter and Steven C. Hawthorne; Pasadena: William Carey Library, 1999) 63.

4. Christoph Blumhardt in Jürgen Moltmann, "The Hope for the Kingdom of God and Signs of Hope in the World: The Relevance of Blumhardt's Theology Today," *Pneuma: The Journal of the Society for Pentecostal Studies* 26/1 (Spring 2004): 8.

5. Ibid.

6. Rob Bell, interview, *Relevant* 31 (January–February 2008): 67.

7. Blumhardt in Moltmann, "The Hope for the Kingdom of God and Signs of Hope in the World," 6.

8. Ibid., 9.

9. Walter Wink, *The Powers that Be: Theology for a New Millennium* (New York: Doubleday, 1998) 95–96.

10. Chris Marshall, "A Prophet of God's Justice: Reclaiming the Political Jesus," *Stimulus* 14/3 (August 2006): 35.

11. Ibid., 40.

12. James L. Boyce, "Hearing the Good News: The Message of the Kingdom in Mark," *Word & World* 26/1 (Winter 2006): 37.

Chapter 8

The Posture of Creative Responsibility

There is no time for cut-and-dried monotony. There is time for work. And time for love.

—Gabrielle Chanel[1]

I am in the middle of doing our family laundry right now. I can see two piles of laundry staring me in the face at this moment. In fact, the dryer just buzzed telling me it's finished with its current load, but I'm going to keep writing anyway. Laundry is one of those completely uninspiring aspects of my life. Others may be called forth to it, may yearn to do it, and may enjoy the fact that something that once was dirty now is clean with a mere whoosh of a Whirlpool. I am not one of those people. My mother is an amazing presser; I don't know if she loves to do it or not, but she irons just about everything that comes out of the dryer *as* it comes out. She irons things *before* they go into the closet. This, I've discovered, is not a genetic trait.

For me, there is no satisfaction in laundry, simply because it is always there to do. There are only three members of my family, and I feel as though I do laundry constantly; I can't imagine what a family of six or eight people goes through. If I walked through my house and actually saw all the laundry hampers in it were empty, I'd know to get right with Jesus because the end of all things would surely come soon.

I found myself in a laundry rut not too long ago. You know the feeling: you are trying to finish something you must do repeatedly, but it is completely uninspiring. We must do some tasks each day, each week, or each year that involve little or no creativity. You could do such a task, or your friend could do it, and it wouldn't make much difference; in the end, you get clean clothes no matter who puts the detergent in and pushes the buttons on the washer and dryer. Whether it is repetitive job tasks, a traffic-congested route to work, or a calendar that never varies from year to year, it adds up to a monotonous routine that keeps you from adventurously springing out of bed in the morning.

Do all these activities in our lives—doing the laundry, mowing the grass, sifting through the bottomless in-boxes in our offices—serve some purpose? Can we actually be thankful for the opportunities in the mundane? Can the monotony in our lives be redeemed?

I recently participated in a Bible study examining the book of Ruth. The discussion was about how God has everything under control, how he holds the big, eternal view and we humans don't see the big picture. This is true, we all nodded and agreed like a good Sunday school class, and yet I thought to myself, this seems to be one of those truths that Christians assent to mentally but don't always *feel* the effects of daily. If we confidently recognized God's purpose and plan each day, and felt as though we were a part of it, how would the little things we do each day be different? Would we do them differently? Would the monotony in our lives be redeemed?

The brief but beautifully written tale of Ruth describes a woman who, though she has lost her husband, joins her fate to that of her mother-in-law and journeys to a country she doesn't know. They are both destitute and have no means of living, so Ruth humbles herself and assumes the posture of a beggar. She picks up the leftover grain behind the harvesters in farmer Boaz's field. In a wonderful irony, Boaz is a distant relative who is able to bring the two women back into "good" society by marrying Ruth. The story ends as most happy stories do, with the birth of a child, a son who extends the line of the family.

Through the ages, Ruth has been hailed as an example of faithfulness for her devotion to her mother-in-law. She, however, is not the only one in the story whose faithfulness deserves mention. Boaz, after all, was a farmer. He did the day-in and day-out work of overseeing crops and workers, planning and planting. He did this day after day, year after year. He saw the rhythm of the seasons, the way the earth and sky work in unity to create sustenance. He knew the labor and the sacrifice needed to yield life. He knew that there was work to do, but that ultimately, an element of grace was involved in each harvest. His was not the only hand put to his fields.

Boaz was faithful, not only in the labor of his harvest, but also in his daily, yearly *methods* of harvesting. Levitical law guided the Hebrews in their farming methods, something that might seem surprising to us today. After all, we don't find instructions in the Bible on how to design a webpage or advice on the best time to launch our own businesses. But Boaz, we know, was faithful to Levitical law, even in his daily work as a farmer. The book of Ruth does not say he bowed down to fertility gods or rubbed his lucky rabbit's foot in order to secure a good harvest. It tells us he was careful to leave the gleanings of his harvest for the marginalized of society as God's Law advised him (see Lev 23:22): "When you reap the harvest of your land, do not reap the very edges of your field or gather the gleanings of your harvest. Leave them for the poor and alien."

Surely some years the harvest was abundant, and surely pests or ill weather conditions spoiled it during other years. Surely it would have been easy for Boaz to rationalize such a statement in the law, to convince himself that this applied to other farmers. "I've had a bad year. I'm sure it won't make any difference if I keep all the harvest for myself, just this year." But he didn't. Year after year, harvest after harvest, he left the gleanings of his hard work for those who had not earned it. He did it without recognition simply because God, who had revealed himself as the ultimate provider for his people, asked Boaz to do it. In this act, God provided. As it turns out, one particular harvest was notable, not for its size, but for one humble peasant who found herself the grateful recipient of wheat she didn't work for. Boaz's small decision to be obedient provided an opportunity for the realization of God's grace-filled plan. Ruth and her mother-in-law found a kinsman redeemer in Boaz, not because he married Ruth, but because of his willingness to let God's desires shape the way he worked every day, every year.

What is more interesting about Boaz's small, repetitive act of faithfulness is that its effects were not limited to his own life and his own family. We find in Matthew 1 that both Boaz and Ruth are part of the lineage of Jesus, one more reminder generations later of the way a posture of obedience can stir the opportunity for grace to move. Could it be that God's purposes might someday redeem the monotony in *our* lives? If that is the case, how might we live differently? Can we think about our tasks in a new way? Can we dive into each day with first-day-of-school excitement? Can we be fueled by the hope and opportunities before us? Can we find meaning and creativity in the mundane?

We also get in ruts, it seems, due to repetition. Maybe what we're doing is completely creative and stimulating the first time, but after a thousand times, the task ceases to be what it once was. How can you refuel when, in the office, you are asked to host the same meetings week after week, year after year? Or is it that you were excited about the sample product, but mass production drove away any inspiration you gained from your original piece? How can we reclaim the monotony in our lives when our creative fruit is squeezed dry of its juices?

Recently, I met a man, John, who is a metalworker, a modern-day blacksmith. He told me about how he went to school, studied biology, and planned to work in the field of genetics. At some point along the way, he encountered a man from Germany who was a metalworker, and, after spending a weekend with him, John fell in love with metalworking himself and knew he wanted to spend his life doing it. He began to learn his craft, and now he has his own shop where he creates lovely ironwork. This, to me, sounded like an incredibly beautiful life. Even now, I envision myself doing something like that, complete with a soundtrack of French music playing. I can see myself now, rising each morning to the chirping of the birds, stretching as I go to my workshop in the back of the house to create beautiful pieces of art with my hands; surely all who saw them would want at least six for themselves. *What a great life*, I thought. John's office is one in which he gets to work with his hands to create tangible art every single day.

Then, however, John pulled the plug on the French music in my head as he described one year in which he spent *eight months* working on a pair of bronze doors for a client's home. Eight months, day in and day out, working on the same two doors. All day, every day, working on the same two doors. I have to think that, if he's anything like me, at some point he grew bored with the doors. Maybe he started to loathe those doors. If he's anything like me, he probably began secretly wishing the doors would suddenly drop through the workshop floor, and he could stand there for a minute, scratch his head, shrug his shoulders, and then begin something else much more interesting. Maybe he covered his eyes with his forearm when he entered his shop each day, as the gleam of the bronze beckoned him to yet another day of work. Or maybe he began to wish he'd designed the doors differently and could start over, or that his clients would've let him do a new design he'd recently devised. The point is, John worked each day on the same pieces of metal for eight months, and while this ultimately was a creative act, it was also an act of *discipline*. As he stood there and told me of his work with the doors, no other word came to mind. Other artists I've spoken with, those who do studio art, photography, and dance, all speak of the fact that creativity has a necessary foundation of discipline. Sometimes, it seems, in life and in faith, creativity and the ability to inspire others ultimately requires discipline. I'm sure the steps in the discipline process become monotonous, no matter what dance you dance or what oil you apply to your canvas. But, as we've seen from the life of Boaz, we never know when God's grace will burst into our efforts, making our hokey-pokeys and our paint-by-numbers something truly breathtaking for his glory.

Several years ago, I read an article that made me think again about the things we are required to do. The author differentiated between passive responsibility, which is basically fulfilling your role, obeying all the rules, and doing your duties in order to finish them, and creative responsibility. Creative responsibility, the article said, "looks beyond one's predefined roles and sees the wider picture: a world in which we are part of the web of life, a world in which we are aware of global interdependence, a world crying out for compassion and transformation."[2] Shouldn't we as followers of Jesus strive for that kind of creativity in our responsibilities? It isn't enough, according to this way of thinking, that we fulfill others' expectations or even God's expectations by checking off a mental list in our heads of how little we can do. Responsibilities aren't only about us. Neither are our lives, for that matter. Are we looking creatively at our Christian lives and praying for new ways to accomplish what we must do? Can we look beyond our predetermined roles as stay-at-home moms, ministers, ad agents, etc., and see what God sees? Do we long for ways to connect with others, to use our daily tasks as opportunities to affect others on a local and global scale? Can we assume a posture of creative responsibility? The article I read says, "Today's global concerns demand that we overcome our conditioning to passivity," and I believe this is true.[3] We are conditioned to do the minimum, even to do many things and merely complete them, giving little thought to how well we do them. The Christian life, however, is not necessarily the same. If we seek God in our monotony, if we let him shape it into discipline, faithfulness, and creative responsibility, we build opportunities where we may witness God's beauty.

Be it laundry or another monotonous task, let us listen to the lives of Boaz, Ruth, and also the apostle Paul, who practiced a posture of creative responsibility even in the monotonous. Paul also must have dealt with monotony, because he warned us in Galatians 6:9 about how easy it is to become weary in doing the good we know we must do. "At the proper time," he reminds us (and could he have been thinking of Boaz?), "we will reap a harvest if we do not give up."[4]

Practicing the Postures

1. Identify the monotonous tasks and responsibilities in your life. Pray and ask God to speak to you about them.
2. Where in your life can you move from passive responsibility to creative responsibility?

Notes

1. Gabrielle Chanel, 10 January 1971, in James B. Simpson, ed., *Simpson's Contemporary Quotations* (Boston: Houghton Mifflin Company, 1988) 4923.

2. Patricia Fresen, "Responsibility and Caring for One Another," in *Responsibility in a Time of AIDS*, ed. Stuart C. Bate (Pietermaritzburg, South Africa: St. Augustine College, 2003) 65–66.

3. Ibid.

4. Since writing this, I've discovered Kathleen Norris and Bonnie J. Miller-McLemore, two other authors you might enjoy, who've written along these same themes.

Chapter 9

The Posture of Expectancy in Worship

It is madness to wear ladies' straw hats and velvet
hats to church; we should be wearing crash helmets.
—Annie Dillard[1]

Do you remember what it was like to open a fresh box of crayons when you were a child? Can you remember the way you would try to carefully perforate the cardboard container, and then slide the top back to reveal the spectrum of perfectly shaped colors? Can you smell that warm, waxy aroma? Do you remember the names of the colors that inspired you? Was it Midnight Blue or Burnt Sienna? "I shall create masterpieces," you thought, "with a thick white pad of paper and this box of new crayons." And you did. The possibilities were endless.

How does it feel to start the New Year? We relish the upcoming possibilities, the opportunities, the challenges. We race to buy new calendars and planner pages with fresh white squares and look ahead to special occasions. How will we fill in these boxes, these days, weeks, months? What will happen to us this year and who will we become? Where will we be, who will we be, at this time next year? What expectations do we have for ourselves, for others, for our lives at the start of a new year?

I feel the same excitement every time I walk into a library or a bookstore. Standing there, I feel almost like a character in one of those "choose your own adventure" books that were popular when I was a child. There I am, hopefully with an hour or two to browse, with just about every imaginable subject at my fingertips. I could make my way to the art books and ponder pointillism. I could find some Robert Frost poems and stop off in a snowy evening. Or I might squeeze myself into a tiny armchair and laugh out loud at a "Ramona" book in the children's area. I can catch up on the latest theories or delve deep into ancient texts. I can flip magazine pages and get a glimpse of the temporary, or I can read a chapter or two of a literary classic. The possibilities are endless, and I almost feel as though I am not merely picking out a book, but exploring the possibilities of who I might one day become.

When do you feel most excited about the possibilities before you? When do you sense that the unexpected could happen to you at any moment, and you know you would absolutely love it? Where are you when the impossible seems possible? What are you doing when your options seem limitless, your potential unfettered? Maybe it is your first day of school, or your moments before a blank canvas. Maybe it is standing seaside as a wave melts the sand beneath your feet. When are you most open to the possibility of what *could be*, and not bound by *what is*? When are you most willing to say, "Come what may"?

Did you happen to answer, "When I'm at church" to one of the questions above? Do you enter worship with a sense of openness, adventure, or expectation? Do you go to church with a willingness to be formed by God, even if it means you will be changed in ways you didn't expect? Does the body of believers with whom you worship on Sunday morning have a sense of expectancy? Do you walk into the building wondering how you'll be different when you exit? Are you reminded at church that the possibilities are endless?

Out of all the places in this world, the church, the body of Christ, should be a place where one is able to catch a glimpse of kingdom possibilities. It is the place where we worship the One who told us repeatedly that, with him, nothing is impossible. In worship, we should seek to find ways we can better experience and participate in the kingdom of God in this life. We should expect to leave having had a taste of who we are, who God is, and who we can be in his grace. We should feel as though we are all thick, fresh tablets of drawing paper and beautiful boxes of sixty-four Crayolas with which he will create masterpieces. His possibilities are endless indeed.

We don't always feel that way when we enter our churches, though, do we? Instead of looking clean and open as they do the first few weeks of January, our lives look like ragged, scribbled-on calendars at the year's end.

We are worn, written in, and blocked off. *What keeps us from a posture of openness and expectancy when we enter the church?*

For some, familiarity lulls us, keeping us from edge-of-our-seats expectancy. We know who will be there, where they will sit, and what Scripture the pastor will use for the sermon. Or we know each verse of the hymns we've been singing since childhood, so we let the words float over us without notice. Routine sets in and then after a while, we forget to engage, simply because it takes more effort to do so in comfortable surroundings. Familiarity can easily keep us in a religious haze, fogging the beauty of kingdom possibilities Sunday after Sunday.

Others are limited each Sunday by the simple fact that the church is made up of people, and with many or most of these people, we have some sort of history. Every Sunday we are surrounded by those who have somehow hindered personal worship; sitting in a pew to your left is the woman who yelled at you during a committee meeting last week, and to the right is a man who cheated your brother in a real-estate deal. Do we forget that we might be a similar hindrance to others?

Some of us have lost the sense of expectancy simply because we are too busy giving and serving at the church itself. Obviously, ministering in Christ's name is something Christ himself commands us to do (John 17). However, when we begin to see our time of worship only as a time of giving and not as a time of receiving from God, our acts become more about self than about God or others. How can giving and serving at church become self-centered? To be sure, we ultimately serve the Lord Christ. I wonder, however, if we as Christ-followers have lost our ability to receive, both from God and from others? Do we settle for the things *we* can accomplish on Sunday mornings instead of awaiting what only *Christ* can bring to our lives?

Another hindrance to openness in worship is an attitude of finality. Many of us walk into church feeling as though everything is settled in our faith lives; we've at some point decided to follow Christ, and so everything is taken care of and done. We've shrunk a life's faith journey into a salvific acrostic, a decision and a prayer, the whole of which results in a five-minute transaction. True, faith decisions sometimes need only seconds, and, true, there is a point in one's life when he or she chooses to follow Christ or not. Sometimes, however, the comforting idea that we have done our duty soothes us into a type of faith that isn't, well, faith.

These hindrances to a posture of openness in a life of faith are not exhaustive. Lack of attention, placing doctrine on a pedestal, unwillingness to devote time, apathy, fear . . . . We can think of many other ways we snuff out our expectancy in this life of faith. When we ascribe to God our limited, preconceived ideas of who he is and what he can and can't do, we go about our day by the faint glow of a smoking wick instead of working in the warm light of his dancing flame.

So what is a posture of expectancy in a life of faith, and how does one go about learning to explore and to receive? What can we do to gain or regain a sense of openness to God, of excitement in our faith lives? How can we declare, "Come what may" with our actions?

If you are falling into familiarity in your worship and time with God, it may help to begin to pray for a change of scenery. Many times the Lord uses both literal and figurative changes of scenery to remind us of the true meaning behind the physical tasks of the faith life. He can bring newness of life out of the old (2 Cor 5:17). Also, commit to engaging your mind and your sense of creativity in your time with God. Have you forgotten what a gracious gift the Lord's Supper is? Visit a mass and contemplate the similarities and differences in your experiences. Have you noticed yourself snoozing through sermons of late? Download sermons on your iPod and listen to them while walking by a lake or through a park. Tired of the same old song you sing each week in corporate worship? Research where that song originated, who wrote it, and under what circumstances it was composed. Pushing past the familiar is not only God's task; it may take much effort on your part, but the Lord will grace that effort with his surprising presence. Remember that Jesus, the Son of God, came from Nazareth, a place from which no one thought anything miraculous could come. As we see so many times in Scripture, God delights in using the willing lives of those who might seem ordinary from the outside.

In the same way, we must continually keep grace before us as we worship with others who either contribute to or distract from our concentration on God. There is so much at stake as we continually battle our humanity as assembled believers. We see the temporary and forget to look with grace-filled eyes at others and at our own lives. It is an extremely difficult task to gather together in worship, as we all are trying to connect with the living God while still clothed in the tight threads of humanity. It may be that praying the Jesus Prayer, a historic Orthodox prayer, can help us: "Lord, Jesus Christ, Son of God, have mercy on me, a sinner." Annie Dillard speaks aptly of the miracle of Sunday worship simply because of the grace we have in Christ: "Week after week we witness the same miracle: that God, for reasons unfathomable, refrains from blowing our dancing bear act to smithereens. Week after week, Christ washes the disciples' dirty feet, handles their very toes, and repeats, 'It is all right, believe it or not, to be people.'"[2] Praise be to God that we are believers in the One who overcame his humanity while here on earth and redeemed ours.

Another aspect of the posture of expectancy exists in the practice of silence and solitude before service. Jesus himself modeled this, so much so that the Gospel writers repeatedly note the times he stole away for solitary prayer and reflection (Mark 1:35 and others). It is only fitting, then, that those of us who struggle to receive from God instead of perform for him learn from Christ's example. How much more do *we* need to sit in silence and learn of him? It seems that only when we take time to practice receiving from him do we come to him with expectant joy. As Luke says, if we, who are evil, can do a few good things here and there, how much more can the Heavenly Father do through the pouring out of his Holy Spirit if we ask him to do so (11:13)? We must learn to receive, to sit in silence, to listen to and savor our God.

Further, in striving for openness and possibility in our lives of faith, we must adopt an appreciation for the mysteries of our God and an excitement over the ongoing nature of the journey. Having a few aspects of your faith life "settled" does not earn you a Finished Product Diploma in heaven. Rather, you've now received a passport that gives you the chance to roam the realm of faith, to wander and wonder, to explore and extract. A professor of mine once recommended reading from a Bible without notes or underlining when you need a fresh perspective. In this way, you allow yourself to look with fresh eyes on the text, not repeatedly going back to your old insights, but expecting to receive new ones.

Why would we desire a finished faith life? In actuality, there probably isn't such a thing. Why would we worship a God we can completely predict? Are we so bent on understanding all the mysteries, so bent on wielding our own souls, that we are unwilling to continue the faith journey? It *is easier* to control and to reduce religious matters, and there is a temptation to do so because it is comforting. But then again, is that the life of faith Christ describes for us when he speaks of the kingdom of God? Does that "all-figured-out" life actually *require* faith? I'm grateful that we worship a God who is living and is willing to let us explore him for the rest of our lives. I'm grateful that we will never come to "The End" until we breathe our last, only to find that our life of faith is just beginning.

What paradise we find in possibility! That's what poet Emily Dickinson believed as she wrote the following:

I dwell in Possibility–
A fairer House than Prose–
More numerous of Windows–
Superior–for Doors–

Of Chambers as the Cedars–
Impregnable of Eye–
And for an Everlasting Roof
The Gambrels of the Sky–

Of Visitors–the fairest–
For Occupation–This–
The spreading wide my narrow Hands
To gather Paradise.[3]

May we as followers of Christ continually seek a glimpse of the mansions of possibility that await us.

Practicing the Postures

1. In what areas of your life do you feel that the possibilities are truly endless?
2. Pick one or more of the methods mentioned in the chapter above to encourage your sense of expectancy in worship. Practice that method every time you attend worship in the next month.

Notes

1. Annie Dillard, in Eugene Peterson, *The Contemplative Pastor: Returning to the Art of Spiritual Direction* (Grand Rapids: Eerdmans, 1989) 83.

2. Ibid., 84.

3. Emily Dickinson, 23, *Dickinson* (New York: Alfred A. Knopf, 1993) 41.

Chapter 10

The Posture of Coping...and Hoping

I've pitched my tent in the land of hope. (Acts 2:26)

The last time I saw my grandfather was about two years ago. He knew me when I arrived, but I'm not sure if he recognized me when I left.

I flew to St. Louis, Missouri, on a gray, snowy Saturday. My mother met me at the airport and together we drove an hour south toward a little hospital in southeast Missouri where my Papa (we pronounce it Paw-Paw) was a patient. I headed to this hospital two weeks after Papa was first admitted there. Until that day, Papa stubbornly lived on his own, wanting to die in the same county in which he was born and lived his entire life. Since 2002, when he lost his wife, my mother had driven four-and-a-half hours every other weekend from Kansas City to refill his medications, do his grocery shopping, clean his house, and cook him freezer-friendly meals he could thaw later in the week. One Sunday, she came to town to discover that the cough and cold she'd detected in Papa's voice over the phone had worsened. She took him to the hospital; you don't let a cold get too advanced in an eighty-nine-year-old with diabetes, chronic obstructed pulmonary disease, and congestive heart failure. Together, they made the drive to Jefferson Memorial Hospital where they waited for six hours to be seen by a doctor. "In 1954," Papa said while they waited, "Stella Valley came to my door asking for a donation to build this hospital. I gave her five dollars, and I'm sorry I did it." Papa was diagnosed with pneumonia and admitted for observation.

On Tuesday, the second day of his hospital stay, Papa had a stroke. His doctor, "a good ol' country boy" according to my Papa, said it was a mild one, and it was true. Within the week, Papa regained the ability to walk, talk, and grip items with his right hand just about as well as he did before. On Friday of that week, he was released from the hospital to an assisted living apartment Mom arranged for him. The transition was made carefully; Papa recently had been arguing explosively with my parents over his inability to pass his driver's test, and his inability to live on his own was certainly another painful chip off his quickly shrinking independence. Surprisingly, he admitted to my mother and the hospital social worker that he didn't think he could live on his own anymore. He still didn't want to accept my parents' offer to move in with them in Kansas City, so my mother called some movers and had his things set up in his new assisted living apartment. His new place was called "The Villas," and he knew a few friends of the family there who promised to help him get acclimated.

The social workers at The Villas said it would be a good idea if my mom got him settled in and then let him make his way for a couple of weeks before she came down again. The idea was that Papa was to try his new apartment, complete with bed, mini fridge, sitting area, private bath, and patio, at least through the winter months. Who knew? After a few months of physical therapy, he actually might be able to return home. For now, Papa was happy that his "big chair" had been moved from home to greet him at his new place. "Don't know what else I'd need besides this," he said as he saw his room for the first time.

Except for his hearing aids, which were giving him a hard time, Papa seemed to do well in his new place. One night he couldn't find his way back to his room from the communal dining room, but after living in the same house since 1970, he was bound to get turned around in those long, uniform hallways. We were pleased to hear from the nurses that Papa had sat in the main common area a few evenings instead of sticking to his own room. He loved to visit with people, and this was a good sign. It seemed as though we had all successfully navigated these precarious new waters.

The next Friday, a week after he moved in, my mom received a call from The Villas in the middle of the night. Papa had fallen in his apartment and fractured his right hip. It was grace that this happened while he lived at The Villas, we knew, instead of when he lived alone, but we wondered what this new injury meant. My mom quickly packed, prepared a week's worth of lesson plans for her fourth grade class, and began her familiar drive to

Jefferson Memorial Hospital. As she drove, I booked a flight for the next morning to St. Louis. Papa was to have hip surgery sometime that weekend, once his blood thickened, and I was going up to be with him and Mom.

As we drove toward the hospital that Saturday, I wondered what version of Papa I would see when I arrived. The Papa I had known was tall, thin in the arms and legs, but round through the belly. His coloring was the same no matter the season; it seemed that God had stretched brownish-red leather over his body instead of the skin everyone else got. He'd worked construction jobs in the sun all his life and had scars from third-degree burns he got from the chest up when a radiator exploded on him. I hardly ever remember seeing Papa wearing anything other than blue Dickies workpants and a plaid shirt. He combed his thinning gray hair straight back, and thick glasses always sat atop his misshaped nose, from which skin cancer had been removed multiple times. After he quit smoking, he always carried Certs mints in his front shirt pocket. When I was a child, he let me jump up on his lap and fish one or two out of his pocket. I was Papa's "Baby Doll."

When I walked in, he knew me and asked why I didn't bring his great-granddaughter to see him, which I took as a good sign. I brought a bulky, uncomfortable chair in from the hallway and pulled it up beside his bed, and Mom and I stayed there with him for the next four days. The surgery on his hip went well. We helped him with his meals and tried to get him to talk, but he mainly slept, the only life function he could do on his own.

Wednesday morning, three days after his surgery, we walked into the hospital to find the nurses busy with Papa's discharge papers. We were shocked that someone in such a state *could* be released, but we needed to work quickly through the decision of where he would go next. His doctor didn't think he would be able to make the four-and-a-half-hour trip to my parents' house, even by ambulance. He had to go somewhere locally where he could get rehab for his hip, and also for the life functions he'd lost like eating, walking, etc. The doctor recommended he be transferred to a nursing home around the corner from his home, a step down from the independence he briefly enjoyed at The Villas.

Later that morning, we went to speak with the woman in charge of new admits at the nursing home. She was probably in her sixties, a chain smoker by her voice and smell, and wore a t-shirt decorated with puff paint. She wasn't polite or rude, but she made it known to us that she knew our Papa and knew "how heartbroken he was when they took his car away from him." She gave us a tour of the nursing home, telling us too much of the truth about the facility, the ratios of workers to patients, etc. But Papa couldn't make it anywhere else, his doctor told us, so we signed the papers and moved a small number of things from his apartment to his new room at the nursing home.

It was about that time that I began thinking how much I hated death. This was not news to me, but I began to burn inwardly at what was happening to my Papa. I knew death would come to him someday. In spite of this, I felt completely overcome by how dehumanizing death was, how it stealthily drew near, making a steely man who'd lived through the Depression into one who lacked the strength to hold my hand. I hated death. I hated seeing him like this. And I hated that I couldn't do anything to make it better for him.

I was reminded how much I saw myself as the "fix-it" girl in life, and it wasn't all inordinate pride. Every boss I've ever had has pointed me to a room, a filing system, or even his or her own office and said, "Help me make sense of this." Friends close and not so close have called me about awful circumstances. College students have sat on my couch asking me for advice. Death, however, put a quick end to that prideful trip. Sometimes reality is bloody and soiled—and there is nothing we can do to fix it.

I was reminded of the few coping skills I'd acquired over the years. Nicholas Wolterstorff, in a book he wrote about losing his young son, says, "We live in a time and place where, over and over, when confronted with something unpleasant, we pursue not coping but overcoming. Often we succeed. Most of humanity has not enjoyed and does not enjoy such luxury."[1] He's right. Most of the circumstances we face day in and day out here in the West are aspects of life that we have some control over, some ability to change. I had to figure out, however, how to live in light of this change in Papa in a way that didn't allow death's advance in me. I had to figure out how to cope *and* hope.

I love what Madeline L'Engle writes about her mother's decline and death: "I rebel against death, yet I know that it is how I respond to death's inevitability that is going to make me less or more fully alive."[2] How I cope, I realized, determines how I live and experience life, even in the face of this reality.

Hope, it seems, is not bubbly ignorance of the truth but a view of the world that takes reality into account. Reality and hope are not mutually exclusive, but rather deepen and enrich each other. I learned this truth at an art exhibit I once attended at the Durban Art Gallery in South Africa.

Hanging on the walls were outlines of about fifty people who were HIV positive, traced by another person while the individuals were lying on the paper. Then, each person had gone back and added elements to the outline that individualized it. Did the person wear glasses? Did she have a chipped tooth? Did he or she have scars? Where and what from? Further, each person had added words and pictures, depicting personality, history, and emotions.

I stood there at length reading the self-descriptions to the side of each drawing. The exhibit was amazing; I was literally seeing portraits of lives in front of me. Violence and abuse marked some of the physical bodies; others had a proud smile that was said to resemble a family member's. Some wore dancing shoes; some bore lyrics to their favorite music; and others had knots or fire in their stomach to symbolize the pain of their symptoms. Life had literally marked these people.

The truth is, we have all been marked by life and the lives of others. It would be silly to act like hope makes the difficult realities of life disappear, that having faith in Christ takes it all away. It would be a lie. Nicholas Wolterstorff, the author mentioned above, writes, "In my living, my son's dying will not be the last word. But as I rise up, I bear the wounds of his death. My rising does not remove them. They mark me."[3] We still see the scars life has given us. They may change or fade, but our wounds go with us through this life. We still have pain. We still have to bury our Papas, and we still cry later when we find the handwritten hospital donation receipt he saved for fifty years.

So how do we live, marked by the past, wrestling with the present, and wielding no control over the future? How do we live true to our history and fully present today, not wishing for an escape? Is hope irrelevant? Irrational? Unrealistic?

Theologian Jürgen Moltmann writes, "The believer is not set at the high noon of life, but at the dawn of a new day at the point where night and day, things passing and things to come, grapple with each other."[4] I think this is a fancy way of saying what orphan Annie knew as a kid: "The sun'll come out . . . tomorrow." Whichever version you prefer, doesn't it ring with truth? Just because I'm a Christian does not mean my life is all fun-in-the-sun noonday. No, it's more like dawn, when I still feel the effects of night and yet strain to see a glimpse of light ahead. We don't live each day outside of history, but we grapple with the present day, living out of our histories and into the possibilities for the future.

The writer of the book of Hebrews uses similar imagery. In Hebrews 6:18, the NRSV calls those who follow Christ refugees who are strongly encouraged to seize the hope set before them. I read this verse one morning recently and didn't think much of it. Later that day, I attended a meeting with an amazing lady who directs extensive programs that daily help thousands of immigrants in the Kansas City area. She told us the majority of the people she serves are from nations at war, and that most of them literally have walked with their families and a few precious belongings across the border of their country to refugee camps they'd heard about. After waiting days or weeks to be processed, the people in the U.S. refugee camps are put on a plane and brought to Kansas City, where her organization helps them begin life in an unknown place.

Immediately, the Scripture I'd read that morning came alive. The faces of the immigrants gave me a picture of Christ-followers as those who are journeying, stepping out beyond what is known. We're traveling a long, exhausting road to a life we never knew existed. "To believe," says Moltmann,

> does in fact mean to cross and transcend bounds, to be engaged in an exodus. Yet this happens in a way that does not suppress or skip the unpleasant realities. Death is real death, and decay is putrefying decay. Guilt remains guilt and suffering remains, even for the believer, a cry to which there is no ready-made answer. Faith does not overstep these realities into a heavenly utopia, does not dream itself into a reality of a different kind. [5]

We're not transported to a place of bliss; we're refugees taking step after step after step toward a place we've heard about but not seen. We're not denying our past, but carrying it with us as we dare to discover a different life ahead. As Fred Craddock says, "We who flee are not scattered aimlessly by fear; rather, we move deliberately toward the hope lying before us."[6]

And isn't it a temptation to get tired of the traveling? Isn't it tiring to put one foot after another only to awaken to another day of the journey before you? It's exhausting, to be sure. But what do we risk by despairing, by giving up hope of new life just beyond the border? If we aren't willing to hope, to keep walking, to keep grappling with the night behind us or reaching for the light just ahead, death is certain. So we keep walking. "That we do not reconcile ourselves, that there is no pleasant harmony between us and reality, is due to our unquenchable hope," writes Moltmann.[7]

What if the "something" we reach out for turns out to be nothing? What if we're walking toward a mirage? What if we awaken to another long day of traveling and don't feel hopeful? Praise be to God that hope is much more than how we feel on a given day. It exists outside of us; it is an entity in itself. It is the essence of Jesus' message and his life within us. I like what Fred Craddock's commentary says about the Hebrews passage:

> Like faith, hope is a primary ingredient of a life healthy and alive toward God. But the contribution of 6:18-20 to our thinking about hope is that it is presented *not so much as our posture toward God and the future as it is a quality of the Christian message,* real and certain in itself, however we may happen to feel on any given day. Hope is out in front of the refugees, beckoning them. Hope is an anchor firm and secure in the very place where God is. Hope has already entered the inner sanctuary, where the act of atonement is offered and received. We must have hope to be sure, but *on occasions when we feel no hope, hope still exists.*[8]

Hope is more than what we feel. We long to feel hopeful, but in the times when we can't assume a posture of hope, we cope, knowing hope still exists, beckoning us from beyond. So then, as the writer of Hebrews later encourages us, "Let us hold fast to the confession of our hope without wavering, for he who has promised is faithful."[9]

The "he" in that verse is not just any "he," but Jesus himself. What a difference it makes that Jesus, the Son of God, is with us in our grappling with night and day! What a grace to know that he grapples against night as well. Moltmann says this:

> The raising of Christ is not merely a consolation to him in a life that is full of distress and doomed to die, but it is also God's contradiction of suffering and death, of humiliation and offence, and of the wickedness of evil. Hope finds in Christ not only a consolation *in* suffering, but also the protest of the divine promise *against* suffering.[10]

I like the version below even better. It's a story by C. S. Lewis about a boy, Digory, whose mother is dying. Digory meets Aslan the Lion on an adventure in the magical world of Narnia, and they have this conversation:

> "Son of Adam," said Aslan. "Are you ready to undo the wrong that you have done to my sweet country of Narnia on the very day of its birth?"

"Well, I don't see what I can do," said Digory. "You see, the Queen ran away and—"

"I asked, are you ready," said the Lion.

"Yes," said Digory. He had had for a second some wild idea of saying "I'll try to help you if you'll promise to help about my Mother," but he realized in time that the Lion was not at all the sort of person one could try to make bargains with. But when he had said "Yes," he thought of his Mother, and he thought of the great hopes he had had, and how they were all dying away, and a lump came in his throat and tears in his eyes, and he blurted out:

"But please, please—won't you—can't you give me something that will cure Mother?" Up till then he had been looking at the Lion's great front feet and the huge claws on them; now, in his despair, he looked up at its face. What he saw surprised him as much as anything in his whole life. For the tawny face was bent down near his own and (wonder of wonders) great shining tears stood in the Lion's eyes. They were such big, bright tears compared with Digory's own that for a moment he felt as if the Lion must really be sorrier about his Mother than he was himself.

"My son, my son," said Aslan. "I know."[11]

Praise be to God that Christ knows each step of our journey, each difficulty with which we grapple, and chooses to walk with us along the way.

As I learn about hope, I've found that I'm a human label-maker. Maybe it comes from my organizational side, but I love to get papers in order and put them in a labeled file or to organize the garage in matching storage tubs, all clearly labeled with what's inside. This is a great way to have an organized life, but I'm finding that it is no way to live. What I mean is that labeling aspects of life like "bad relationship" or "annoying boss" is too final. It closes off possibility when the hope of Christ asks us to leave the door open for change and opportunity. It's kind of like what they say about parenting: if you tell your kids they're naughty kids all the time, they will likely begin to fulfill that expectation. If I label aspects of my life, thinking, "This is how it always will be," it probably *will* always be that way.

In reality, we don't see all there is to see. Life as a Christ-follower is so much more than the sum of the parts. Hope is not presumption or pie in the sky by and by, but a passion for the possible, as Moltmann says. If we recognize that life is always changing and progressing, we see that we shouldn't use judgments, but anticipations. Instead of saying, "This is not right," we say, "This is not right *yet*" because, thank God, there is room for growth, room for love. "In its hope," Moltmann says, "love surveys the open possibilities of history."[12]

And so we continue to walk toward that border, willing to leave the dark night behind for a dawning ahead. We take step after step, claiming Psalm 143:8: "Let the morning bring me word of your unfailing love, for I have put my trust in you."[13] We don't know what kind of life awaits us. All we know is that traveling and learning to live life at our destination could be the hardest thing we've ever had to do. But one thing is sure: ultimately, we will leave death behind us for the light up ahead.

Practicing the Postures

1. Are there aspects of your life with which you simply have to cope? What are they? Bring these before the Lord in prayer.
2. Have you recently tired of walking toward the dawn up ahead? Talk to the Lord about this.

Notes

1. Nicholas Wolterstorff, *Lament for a Son* (Grand Rapids: Eerdmans, 1987) 72.

2. Madeleine L'Engle, *The Summer of the Great-Grandmother* (Farrar, Straus & Giroux, 1974; repr., New York: HarperCollins, n.d.) 29.

3. Wolterstorff, *Lament for a Son*, 93.

4. Jürgen Moltmann, *Theology of Hope* (Minneapolis: Fortress Press, 1993) 31.

5. Ibid., 19.

6. Fred B. Craddock, "The Letter to the Hebrews," *The New Interpreter's Bible: A Commentary in Twelve Volumes*, vol. 12 (Nashville: Abingdon Press, 1995) 81.

7. Moltmann, *Theology of Hope*, 22.

8. Craddock, "The Letter to the Hebrews," 83, italics mine.

9. Hebrews 10:23, NRSV.

10. Moltmann, *Theology of Hope*, 21.

11. C. S. Lewis, *The Magician's Nephew* (New York: Macmillan, 1955, repr. New York: Scholastic, 1988) 141–42.

12. Moltmann, *Theology of Hope*, 32.

13. This verse from the NIV.

Chapter 11

The Posture of Hospitality: The Interpersonal Level

> Certainly let the board be spread and let the bed be dressed for the traveler; but let not the emphasis of hospitality lie in these things.
>
> —Ralph Waldo Emerson[1]

I'm nearsighted. I wear glasses or contacts pretty much all the time. I can read the alarm clock in the middle of the night, though, and even when I wake up, I can usually do fine without my glasses for a while. The rooms in our house are small enough that I don't notice the blurriness much when I look across them. My husband and daughter always groan and roll their eyes because, many times, we'll be pulling out of the driveway in the family car before I notice I'm not wearing them. "My glasses!" I'll usually shriek, and then I'll have to open the house back up and retrieve them. I do fine making out objects when I'm in my own home, but the moment I first glance at the sky or a tree across the street, I realize I've only focused on things right in front of me.

Aren't we all a little myopic at times? When it comes to day-in, day-out life, do we focus more on what we need to accomplish instead of where we are and who is with us? Do we forget that we're actually interacting with *real* people?

My mother was an elementary school teacher for many years, and as a child, I always found it funny when we met a student of hers at the grocery store or somewhere else around town. Most of the time, the student stared in a state of shocked silence until he or she could mumble something like, "*You* go to Wal-Mart, *too*?" It was as if they were surprised Mom was a real person instead of someone who lived at the school and existed solely for the purpose of educating them each day. Such a thought from a young child is excusable; living your life this way as an adult is not, especially if you call yourself a Christian. As Donald Miller said once when I heard him speak, "The world is not just a movie about your life, starring you."[2]

The Bible says the same thing (see 1 Pet 4:9), and Jesus' behavior underscores that it is not okay when God's people use others or approach them in a utilitarian fashion. Jesus took time to notice people. He observed a widow donating all her coins, an insecure bully up in a tree, a bunch of men as "holy" as whitewashed tombs. Just because he was God and all-knowing doesn't mean he didn't take the time to notice people while he lived on earth. Maybe he modeled this behavior specifically for us. Whatever the reason, it is clear he engaged those around him. Jesus took time to listen to them and truly know them. Maybe that's why people liked being around him.

Are we who call ourselves Christ's followers emulating Jesus in this way? Are we listening to people, or are we merely waiting for them to stop talking so *we* can talk? Are we taking time to observe, evaluate, and respond to the people in our lives, or have we set our own courses for life and then switched on the autopilot? Jesus showed us true Christian hospitality. He didn't have a tastefully decorated guest wing that he shared with others; he shared himself. He was interpersonally hospitable.

Are we Christians concentrating on living beyond ourselves? Are we nearsighted, seeing only what's right in front of us, as I do without my glasses? Let's face it: we all think we are generous, unselfish people, ready to drop everything for someone who might need us. But *are* we? Are we consistently challenging ourselves to intentionally think outside our own lives? Are we taking time to engage people occasionally, or are we pushing ourselves to be hospitable moment by moment?

"For Christians," says author Paul Wadell, "hospitality is not an occasional gesture, but a whole way of being."[3] This kind of hospitality, Jesus' hospitality, requires that we intentionally live beyond ourselves, engaging others beyond our personal expectations or needs. Christ calls us to live with our world family in mind. He calls us to create space for guests in our lives.

Henri Nouwen talks about creating this kind of "interpersonal space" for others in his book, *The Wounded Healer*. Hospitality, he says, "asks for the creation of an empty space where the guest can find his own soul."[4] What do you do when you prepare a guest room for someone who will enter your home? You clean clutter off the dresser so the guest can put his or her things there. You push your clothes aside in the closet, providing space and extra hangers for the guest's clothes. You replace sheets and towels with freshly washed linens. And, if you're like my mother-in-law, you leave a basket of your guest's favorite snacks by the bed. Henri Nouwen is saying people who enter your life are similar to houseguests. You withdraw part of yourself in order to create space for the other person. We can do this every day in little ways, even in the simplest of interactions.

Sometimes, though, we don't want to create space for others. We have things to do or things we need another person to do for us, or we have things to say on our cell phones. We're unwilling to move the clutter of our lives aside, and guess what? Our guests notice. They see when they're trumped by our "to-do" lists, and they feel interpersonally "unwelcomed." Nouwen says of our reaction toward our "guest,"

> As soon as our intentions take over, the question no longer is, "Who is he?" but, "What can I get from him?"—and then we no longer listen to what he is saying but to what we can *do* with what he is saying. Then the fulfillment of our unrecognized need for sympathy, friendship, popularity, success, understanding, money or a career becomes our concern, and instead of paying attention to the other person we impose ourselves upon him with intrusive curiosity.[5]

Are we Christ-followers imposing ourselves on people in our world, or are we engaging them? Are we challenging ourselves to ask, "Who is he?" or "How can I put her at ease?"

We must create space for guests in our schedules. We've got to slow down our lives. I knew a youth minister who always said, "If you're too busy to spend time with God, then you're busier than he intends you to be." I think Jesus would give this statement a good Baptist "Amen!" and then follow it by saying, "And if you're too busy to spend time with other people, you're too busy as well." After all, what does he say is the first and greatest commandment? Mark 12:28-31 tells us: "'You shall love the Lord your God with all your heart, and with all your soul, and with all your mind, and with all your strength.' The second is this, 'You shall love your neighbor as yourself.' There is no other commandment greater than these." What Christian wouldn't agree with the importance and centrality of these statements in the Christian life? Yet how many times do our actions shrug these commandments aside? We must intentionally anticipate guests in our lives. "Hospitality," says Joan

Chittister, "is one of those things that has to be constantly practiced or it won't be there for the rare occasion."[6]

We must slow down and *listen.* "If there is any posture that disturbs a suffering man or woman," says Henri Nouwen, "it is aloofness."[7] I always think about a certain professor I knew who was a favorite among the students. She wasn't a lecturer and didn't teach classes, but I frequently heard students talk about how great she was. After a thirty-minute conversation with her, I knew why students felt that way. I walked out of her office and shortly realized that the entire time, she focused directly on me, listened to me, and asked me questions about what I was saying. This professor taught me how amazing it feels when you are truly *heard,* and it seems people who were with Jesus felt the same way. Shouldn't we as his followers help other people to feel "heard" as well? I love what pastor and author Eugene Peterson says about the way he evaluates himself: "Speaking to people does not have the same personal intensity as listening to them. The question I put to myself is not 'How many people have you spoken to about Christ this week?' but 'How many people have you listened to in Christ this week?'"[8]

We must also *be willing to risk hospitality.* Why is it easier to ask a family to meet at a restaurant instead of inviting them to your home for a meal? There are many reasons. It's safer when you're first getting to know each other, they won't see that stain on the carpet in the living room, and they won't stay longer than you want them to. Maybe they'll even buy their own meals and it won't cost you anything extra. Restaurants make dining easier for everyone.

Interpersonally, however, God asks us to risk a little more, to open not just our homes but our lives to each other. We must be willing to let the other person know us, to see even the cobwebs in the corners of our hearts, because this is the essence of Christian hospitality. "Hospitality," says Thomas Reynolds, "is not without risk. It involves a mixing between guest and host that undoes the distinction between outsider and insider. Doors swing open and strangers are welcomed as part of the household . . . . In this, the generosity of hospitality consents to a kind of role reversal that now leaves the host vulnerable and dependent as well."[9]

We need to fearlessly be who we are with each other. We need to let outsiders in and let go of our expectations. Yes, it will cost us something, but the sense of interdependence and gratitude we will gain is greater if we take the risk of intentionally engaging those around us. "The primary aim of the Christian life is not to feel safe, but to be faithful," says Paul Wadell.[10]

In faith, we step forward, willing to risk, willing to put aside our intentions in order to make people feel "at home" with us. Hospitality is not just part of faith; it is the motivation for it. *We live hospitably because we've first received.* God's hospitality should not cease in the earthly here and there of our human lives; it should flow through our lives like a fresh breeze on those who've not yet run in the wide-open spaces of God's love. Hospitality comes from "an acknowledgement of being graced, of having been given something to offer. Hospitality is built upon the premise that a host can and should give because she or he has first received."[11] We don't practice hospitality to point other people to ourselves, our church, or even our beliefs. We practice hospitality to point people toward the ultimate welcome that God gives every person through Christ.

It is easy for me to walk around my house, focusing on objects that are only a few feet away. It doesn't strain my eyes much. I could probably live without glasses altogether if I only tried to see things immediately in front of me. But how much would I miss by never venturing beyond myself? How thankful I am that my correctives help me see redbud trees in the spring and the blue ocean that fades into the horizon. Being able to see the world as God meant me to see it is worth every minute required to put my contacts in or go back inside the house for my glasses.

Somehow, this reminds me to ask the Holy Spirit to be the corrective for my nearsighted heart, to keep me from settling for life that's only about what's inches in front of my face. May we strive for a view of the kingdom horizon and work to embody the divine hospitality in which we live.

Practicing the Postures

1. Each time you come into contact with someone this week, notice and engage that person in conversation. Realize that his or her job is not just to bag your groceries or take your complaint over the phone, but that this is a real person with a history and a life. Take note of the lives you encounter on a frequent basis. Notice how this perspective changes your week.

2. Is your schedule so full that you don't have time even for the briefest conversation with another person? Reflect on how you allot your time and whether or not the Lord is leading you to clear the clutter in your schedule to create time for random people you encounter.

Notes

1. *The Works of Ralph Waldo Emerson, Vol. 3* (New York: Hearst's International Library Co., 1914) 285.

2. Donald Miller, lecture at Baylor University, 19 September 2005.

3. Paul J. Wadell, "Toward a Welcoming Congregation," *Christian Reflection* 25 (2007): 77.

4. Henri J. M. Nouwen, *The Wounded Healer* (New York: Doubleday, 1979) 92.

5. Ibid., 90, italics mine.

6. Joan Chittister, in Christine D. Pohl and Pamela J. Buck, "Hospitality and Family Life," *Journal of Family Ministry* 18/3 (Fall 2004): 11–25.

7. Nouwen, *The Wounded Healer*, 71.

8. Eugene H. Peterson, *The Contemplative Pastor: Returning to the Art of Spiritual Direction* (Grand Rapids: Eerdmans, 1989) 21.

9. Thomas E. Reynolds, "Welcoming without Reserve? A Case in Christian Hospitality," *Theology Today* 63/2 (July 2006): 197.

10. Wadell, "Toward a Welcoming Congregation," 79.

11. Reynolds, "Welcoming without Reserve? A Case in Christian Hospitality," 197.

Chapter 12

The Posture of Hospitality: The Corporate Level

And why should the divine hospitality cease here?
—E. M. Forster[1]

We sat in our one-room flat waiting for the phone to ring, for a knock on the door, an e-mail, anything. My husband and I were alone, just a week into our move to South Africa. We had just taken the one family we knew in the country, the Housers, to the airport; they were only visiting the States for two weeks, but it felt like we had watched them board a rocket ship back to our home planet. Matt and I had a car, a book of city maps, a phone book, and all sorts of places we wished to explore. So we did. We scheduled meetings with nonprofits, visited museums, and ate great food. Oh, and we got lost. A lot. Nothing, however, could speak louder than the silence of our flat in the evenings. We wondered, "Where are we?" and "Does anyone know we're here?" We were visitors. We were foreigners.

Then the phone rang. We heard the voice of a South African woman on the other end. Her name was Jenny, and she was someone we finally recognized as an acquaintance of the Housers whom we'd met the week before. She wanted to invite us to a knitting circle of senior adult women that met at her church the next morning. We looked at each other, eyebrows raised. We were in our twenties, neither of us knit, we had no idea how to get there, and Matt would likely find no men at the meeting. Then we looked around at our flat and our empty calendar for the next day. "We'll be there," we told Jenny.

The morning stands out in my mind, but not because of the knitting circle itself. Imagine lots of older South African voices saying, "No, no, *no*, girl! Not *that* way, you must bring the wool *over* the needle next!" Then visualize a neon orange patch of snaggled knitting that my husband dubbed a fine scarf of which any hamster would be proud. It wasn't the knitting circle that makes me remember that day, but another invitation that proceeded from it. For, while I was entangled in my knits and purls, an elderly black woman asked if we had found a church to attend. When I answered no, she invited me to attend hers, an Anglican church called St. Luke's. "We have several masses each Sunday," she said. "I go to the early morning mass, which is traditional, but there are all different kinds. There's one held in Zulu in the afternoon, and one in the evening, but"—and here she scowled—"that one has a lot of loud music, you know." She pretended to strum a guitar and shook her head.

That air guitar mass sounded like just the thing my husband and I would attend. We went the next Sunday. The small assembly in the dark stone chapel was warm and inviting, even to these Texas Baptists who were ten seconds behind every congregational response or time of kneeling. The worship was moving, the homily convicting, and the people welcoming.

However, when it came time for the Eucharist at the end of the service, Matt and I had another conversation with our eyebrows. Should we partake, going forward to the kneeling bench like everyone else? Or should we sit there in the pews? We didn't know if Communion was open or closed to us as Baptists, and as we tried to decide, someone dismissed the row in front of us. Our time to go was coming, and we weren't sure what to do. We wanted to take Communion, but we didn't want to cause a problem. Obviously the priest giving us the elements would know we weren't a part of his parish, and we didn't want him to refuse us the elements in front of everyone. We decided to stay in our row. After all, we were foreigners, culturally and religiously.

Then someone hugged my neck from the pew behind us. It was Jenny, who had sneaked up a few rows, not too quietly, during the Eucharist. While we tried to go unnoticed, Jenny said to us joyfully, "It's okay for you to go up there. We just think that if you love Jesus, you can partake." The priest, not oblivious to the commotion, stopped what he was doing and said simply, "It is the Lord's table, not the church's."

The welcoming we received as we took the elements choked me up (and it wasn't just the real wine in the common cup). This church showed two cultural and religious outsiders loving hospitality. And it continued to do so, whether it was the way one of its home groups took us into its study or the way the worship leader said, "Prayer at the front, coffee at the back," at the end of each mass. The priest himself, a man named Simon, had tea with us, shared books with us, and invited us to say evening prayers with him. He was not trying to impress his tradition upon us or groom us for a position in his parish. He taught us about his faith and his life in South Africa. He invested in us, even though we were strangers who, in all probability, would never return.

I learned from the people at St. Luke's that welcoming the stranger is central in calling yourselves Christians. Churches must have a hospitable response to "the other," and it begins by recognizing, as God reminded the Israelites again and again, that we've all been aliens at one time or another. Exodus and Leviticus contain numerous reminders about treating foreigners with gracious love and all of them end with the phrase "for you were aliens in Egypt."[2] Remember, God says, how it feels to be a stranger in a foreign land. What is more, God called the Israelites themselves *his* aliens, tenants of the land he had given them.[3] Welcoming people totally other than yourselves is something we do because God has done it and is doing it now, with us. Further on in the Christian story, we see hospitality is central to the Jesus-following church. It was a requirement of bishops, even during times when taking strangers into their homes and churches was a physical risk to themselves and others. The book of Third John, an entire letter about receiving others, says that by extending hospitality to strangers we make the faith visible.[4] We read in Hebrews and in the story of Abraham how we should welcome others, even when we don't see the whole picture. God reveals himself in those kinds of moments because they are full of possibility. He isn't calling out, "Gotcha! You weren't being hospitable and it turned out to be *me*!" Rather, we see that God calls us to a lifestyle of welcoming the foreign, of holding open the possibility for him to break in and orchestrate the impossible among us.

Instead of practicing *philoxenos*, which means loving the stranger, we find many times that the church is *xenophobic*, afraid of the differences we find in others. We forget that Jesus, whom we claim to follow, was the ultimate lover of the otherness in people. Even differences in religion didn't freak Jesus out when it came to loving people. Consider this idea from Barbara Brown Taylor:

Because I first learned their stories in church and have heard them there so often, it is often hard to remember that the Greeks, Romans, Canaanites and Samaritans who crossed paths with Jesus were not cardboard characters set up to make him look good. They were religious aliens in the land who did not worship Israel's God. Some of them were hostile to Jews, while some Jews treated others with contempt. They all spoke with accents . . . . When he is faced with a mother's love for her sick child, a leper's gratitude for his healing, or a centurion's concern for his ill servant, Jesus cannot seem to stay focused on the religious otherness of these people. He focuses on their humankind-ness instead.[5]

Again, we see the tradition of hospitality all through Scripture, and the Bible calls not only individuals but the whole church to welcome others. In this sense, we're called to mirror the divine hospitality.

This means we don't get to pick those toward whom we act charitably. The opposite of hospitality is what so many churches today display, says Paul Wadell. He describes this temptation this way:

The antithesis of charity is "safe neighbor love," a love that is calculating, selective, and restricted to all those we prefer to love because they are easy to love. Safe neighbor love is easy to practice because it does not ask much of us, least of all that we make space in our lives for those sons and daughters of God who might need our attention, our resources, and our time. Safe neighbor love sets up the barriers and boundaries that God's love works to tear down. Safe neighbor love is a temptation for all of us (and all too often a habit), but it sabotages the fearless and expansive love of God that inspires true Christian hospitality. And perhaps most importantly, safe neighbor love is at odds with the love we see in God, a love so bold and adventuresome that it entered our world and became one of us in Christ.[6]

Praise be to God that Christ did not shy away from the otherness in us, but gave us the model of loving receptivity.

We must see that Christ calls the church to anticipate the guest, and in doing so, anticipate its own wholeness. We forget in our talk of unity (which devolves into homogeneity) that the "strange" is not a threat to the church, but an opportunity for it. A host, feeling at home in his own house, as Henri Nouwen describes, should work to create freedom for the stranger who happens to find his or her way there.

What does this look like in real life? Let me try to illustrate. Because of his work at a church, my husband and I frequently find ourselves with dinner invitations to the homes of all different ages of people. One night it might be pizza with college students, and the next it might be casserole with a couple in their seventies. While it is refreshing to have my cooking obligations relieved, and I enjoy the conversations at the table, usually the prospect of a meal with someone with no children fills me with dread. Why? Because I know I'm going to spend the evening trying to corral my toddler into an acceptable corner of a pristine house filled with painted ceramic figurines and priceless family memories. I might hear a fragment of conversation, but most of the time, I'm stressed out trying to keep my child (who does the best she can) from ransacking a kid-unfriendly place. Certainly, a couple will tell me to sit down, that it's all right if Lucy explores the house on her own. Then they send her off with an open glass of raspberry Kool-Aid, and you realize this couple hasn't had anyone under the age of forty in their home in decades.

A few weeks ago, I found myself looking ahead to such a night, already dreading an evening filled with "Let's stay away from the Lladros, Lucy," and "It's not a good idea to touch other people's toothbrushes, even if they're left out on the counter." Poor Lucy, who tries her hardest but sometimes seems like the reincarnation of Curious George, had no idea what kind of night was before her—and neither did I. When we arrived, I was delighted to find that our hostess had pulled baskets of her children's old toys from the attic and had them washed and ready for play. Behind the intimidating dining room set with china and crystal stood a child-sized table prepared with kid-friendly dishes. Later, the couple took Lucy out back with them to feed their longhorns, meet the dogs and cats, and explore their property. In every way, they showed us hospitality, simply because they took time to think about who was coming to their home and how they could put us all at ease. I know it required extra preparation on their part, but it made the evening so memorable. We felt loved.

Isn't that what God asks of his church? Romans 12:13 says, "Be inventive in hospitality." Think about who will walk through your doors and what you can do to put them at ease. God asks us not merely to tell people, "You're welcome here anytime," but to *prepare* to do things that will make people feel loved. We must anticipate the guest and his or her needs. The definition of an outsider is that he or she will not "get" everything you do. We need to be ready to bridge that gap with love and flexibility.

This is hard. This is a lot of work. It requires you to open yourself up. Author Thomas Reynolds explains these feelings well:

Once the stranger is invited in, the host yields stability and control, adjusting the household to accommodate and attend to the unique needs of the guest as they become apparent. Offering hospitality in this way invites disruption into the household order and routine. The status quo is challenged. The home is made different, even strange, vis-à-vis the presence of the stranger. The familiar is defamiliarized. Things do not remain intact as they were. The center of gravity shifts.[7]

This should lead us to think hard about what we mean when we say we want to grow our churches. For, ultimately, if we see the body of Christ as a band of believers that gathers together to help each other understand what it means to follow him in this life, Reynolds's paragraph isn't negative. It is exciting. We are asking for more people to come and help us understand our views of faith and life as we journey alongside one another. Our status quo gets challenged. We are longing for new followers of Jesus to bump into our limited understanding of Christianity and show us another way that Jesus is Lord. The center of gravity shifts away from doctrinal differences and leaps toward a dynamic, diverse *life* in Christ.

We don't ask people to come into our little world in order to become just like us. We shouldn't want to grow only to have a bigger circle of people who believe as we do. We want more people through our doors because we believe Jesus Christ has changed our lives, and we want to see how he has—or will—change others' lives as well. How exciting to know that wholeness comes with welcoming the stranger, that God can grow our understanding of him through each new person who walks through the church door. The possibilities abound when people are not merely numbers, are not only "saved" or "lost," but are people whose lives can help our lives in this faith journey we share. Eugene Peterson says this is how God's creation continues: "The streets and fields, the homes and markets of the world are an art gallery displaying not culture, but new creations in Christ."[8] May we as the people of God learn what it means to anticipate the guest and to offer inventive hospitality in Christ's name. May we feel joy in seeing the stranger walk through our doors, so that we might grow together in the fullness of Christ.

Practicing the Postures

1. How does your place of worship anticipate the guest? Does your church see a connection between hospitality and its own wholeness? Why or why not?

2. At my church, we practice the Three Minute Rule at the end of every worship service: take three minutes and talk to someone you don't know. Take time to practice the Three Minute Rule at least once this week as you worship with others.

Notes

1. E.M. Forster, *A Passage to India* (San Diego: Harcourt, 1924) 37.

2. See Exodus 22:21 and Leviticus 19:33-34.

3. Leviticus 25:23.

4. 1 Timothy 3:2; Titus 1:8; and 3 John.

5. Barbara Brown Taylor, "Guest Appearance," *Christian Century* 122/19 (20 September 2005): 37.

6. Paul J. Wadell, "Toward a Welcoming Congregation," *Christian Reflection* 25 (2007): 82.

7. Thomas E. Reynolds, "Welcoming without Reserve? A Case in Christian Hospitality," *Theology Today* 63/2 (July 2006): 197.

8. Eugene H. Peterson, *The Contemplative Pastor: Returning to the Art of Spiritual Direction* (Grand Rapids: Eerdmans, 1989) 6.

Chapter 13

The Posture of Contentment

You is a very fluid concept right now.[1]

—Will Smith in *Hitch*

I've been thinking about contentment a lot lately. I was reading through Luke the other day, when a verse completely stopped me. I couldn't go on reading, and I'm still chewing on it. I'm not sure I know what it means, even now as I write about it. It says, "If you're content to be simply yourself, you will become more than yourself."[2]

I laughed at this verse at first. Content to be yourself? I don't get it. Isn't the whole purpose of religion to be able to transcend yourself, to get beyond the junky, sinful version of you and become the one you were created to be? Doesn't the Bible, not to mention pretty much every sermon we've ever heard, consistently point out where we fall short? Isn't that why we pray, to draw ourselves closer to Christ and let his love transform us moment by moment? What does this translation mean for us about being content with ourselves? If we settle for who we are, aren't we complacent?

If you ask me whether I'm content, I'm sure to tell you yes. I have a great life, an amazing husband, and a cool kid. I've got great family, and I've never wanted for anything much. Sure, I'm content, because how could I ask for more?

But if you followed me around all day and simultaneously saw inside my head, you'd probably hear a different tune. I have a constant song in my head—probably a sad, old country tune—that goes something like, "I shoulda done this better." These lyrics fit every occasion: the awkward conversation ("Did I say something wrong?"), the toddler tantrum ("What could I have done to prevent that? Did I discipline her well?"), and the way-too-baked chicken dinner for ten people ("How could I have forgotten to set the oven timer?"). I'll say I'm fully content, but while I couldn't politely ask for more out of life, I harshly demand more out of myself.

I don't know that this song is all bad. People call it being determined or driven, and the confusing thing is that most everyone will praise you for this quality. You're self-motivated, a self-starter, independent. This relentless "do better" song that plays in my head is a great tune if I spy a problem, because I immediately begin to devise a fix-it plan. Unfortunately, the lyrics blare at me nonstop, even if I've excelled at nine out of ten tasks that day. How can I be "content to simply be myself" when I'm constantly singing another stanza of "Couldn't I have done just a little bit more?"

It seems we're talking about contentment as the opposite of perfectionism. I love what Kathleen Norris says about perfectionism in her book, *Amazing Grace*:

> Perfectionism is one of the scariest words I know. It is a marked characteristic of contemporary American culture, a serious psychological affliction that makes people too timid to take necessary risks and causes them to suffer when, although they've done the best they can, their efforts fall short of some imaginary, and usually unattainable, standard. Internally, it functions as a form of myopia, a preoccupation with self-image that can stunt emotional growth.[3]

Norris speaks of the Christian journey as the willingness to lose that insecure preoccupation with self and walk forward in steps that require us to give of ourselves. "To mature," she says, "is to lose adolescent self-consciousness so as to be able to make a gift of oneself, as a parent, as teacher, friend, spouse . . . . Perfection, in a Christian sense, means becoming mature enough to give ourselves to others."[4]

Are we able to enjoy things as they happen, or are we too preoccupied with getting it right? Do we know how to stop and be content, even if a situation isn't unfolding as we planned? Are we able to be fully present in the moment, realizing its uniqueness? Do we enjoy life as it happens, recognizing that, yes, better days will come, and we can always change something next time? Are we missing the symphony happening all around us because we constantly hum that no-win country ditty to ourselves?

According to Wendell Berry, the answer is in learning how to look past ourselves:

I know for a while again
the health of self-forgetfulness,
looking out at the sky through
a notch in the valley side,
the black woods wintry on
the hills, small clouds at sunset
passing across. And I know
that this is one of the thresholds
between Earth and Heaven,
from which even I may step
forth from my self and be free.[5]

How do we step forth from ourselves in freedom? We learn to look outside ourselves, living in a healthy self-forgetfulness. We embrace each moment, breathing it in. We withhold judgment for a bit, instead looking for what's needed in that particular moment. And we look to God. For over and over again in Scripture, we see that if we look only at ourselves, we will not be satisfied in life. We ultimately cannot satisfy ourselves, but God does satiate us.

The health of self-forgetfulness sometimes means we must take a breath and remember God's priorities are the ones we want to live by, because they'll ultimately give us true life. The Hebrew word *saba*, the word the Bible uses for "satisfied," speaks of the filling and even overfilling of appetites and desires. Repeatedly in the Old Testament, we find Scripture that warns God's people: if they don't follow God's life-giving lifestyle, they'll "eat and not be satisfied."[6] David, the beloved king of God's people, wrote, "My soul is satisfied as with a rich feast," and "You open your hand, satisfying the desire of every living thing."[7] This quest for satisfaction is fulfilled in the person of Jesus Christ; the Gospel writers point to his sustenance by repeatedly telling tales of how Jesus' followers "all ate and were satisfied."[8]

When, then, should we be satisfied with ourselves and our journeys of faith? Maybe we should look at our expectations. Do we expect perfection, or do we expect growth? "To 'be perfect,' in the sense that Jesus means it," says Kathleen Norris, "is to make room for growth, for the changes that bring us to maturity, to ripeness . . . . This sort of perfection demands that we become fully ourselves as God would have us: mature, ripe, full, ready for what befalls us, for whatever is to come."[9] Maybe we need to learn to be as patient with ourselves as we are with others, expecting growth and the blunders that come with life.

It is comforting that when we seek God each day and ask him to work in us, we can trust that he's the one guiding the process of growth. He's the one who gives us what we need to live lovingly through the circumstances of life. We can trust God's work. The apostle Paul knew this. You can see his trust when he writes chapter 4 of his letter to the Philippians, saying, "I've learned by now to be quite content whatever my circumstances . . . . Whatever I have, wherever I am, I can make it through anything in the One who makes me who I am." Paul turns the idea of self-sufficiency upside down, claiming instead to trust in the one who is working to make him who he needs to be in every situation. Further, the verb Paul chooses in this verse to describe God's making and strengthening him gives the idea that God hasn't simply "made" or "strengthened" him at one point, but that God *is now presently* and *continually* giving him the inner and outer resources Paul needs to accomplish his life in love.

What does this mean to you? What does this mean for me? It means I need to remember that life involves process, journey, and change. It means God has made me to be exactly who he needs me to be in order to face the things in front of me. It means that who I am isn't perfect, but that if I ask, God will give me resources to accomplish what he wants me to do. I might not be able to be confident in my actions and abilities 100 percent of the time, but God is constantly shaping me, building in me the things that I lack, and I *can* be confident in *that*. It means that, along with the recognition that there's always work to do, I can acknowledge that God is doing the work. Frederick Buechner says, "In Hebrew peace, *shalom,* means fullness, means having everything you need to be wholly and happily yourself."[10] Praise be that God is working in us to accomplish this wholeness in us, not just for our own happiness, but for his loving purposes.

In chapter 7 of his first letter to the Corinthian church, Paul addresses issues of marriage and how to live in light of a newfound relationship with Christ. He tells them, "Don't be wishing you were someplace else or with someone else. Where you are right now is God's place for you. Live and obey and love and believe right there. God, not your marital status, defines your life." I think this passage speaks to contentment in or outside of marriage, about a sense of being willing to accept our place in our faith life and then continue on in faith, life, and love. What would happen if we began to switch off that country song in our heads and instead began to sing this tune of active acceptance? What would each day be like if we embraced our place on the journey God's guiding us on, not drowning in false guilt, but confidently letting God define our identities as we grow in him?

At the beginning of a recent yoga class, the instructor asked us to close our eyes and set an intention for our practice that day, to decide why we were there and what we wanted to achieve. Then, during the period of quiet at the end of class, she asked us to recall that intention for the class. I enjoy this practice, and here's why: Someday I'd like to be able hold certain yoga poses for ten minutes at a time. I realize, however, that due to tight hamstrings and creaky ligaments, I'm not going to be able to reach that goal all in one class. However, if I'm able to set an intention for growth and change in those postures, I can see that each class that I take is one step closer to realizing my long-term goal. I can take satisfaction in and be thankful for the way my present intentions help me get further down the road.

Isn't that what we need in our daily life as well, to set intentions for ourselves about who we'd like to be, and then later recognize that each day is one day closer to reaching that fullness? We accept ourselves as we go through the growth process, being thankful for the steps in the journey that teach us and make who we are. All the while, God is mysteriously in the mix. Paul knew this mystery, writing to his fellow pastor Timothy about the great gain of godliness combined with contentment.[11] I like the way one translator of this verse speaks of "the rich simplicity of being yourself before God."[12] That's a song we can dance to our whole lives.

Practicing the Postures

1. What helps you know the "health of self-forgetfulness"?
2. Where do you need to remember that God is presently and continually strengthening you for what you face in life?

Notes

1. *Hitch*, DVD, dir. B. Patricia Woodbridge, Columbia Pictures, 2005.

2. Luke 18:14.

3. Kathleen Norris, *Amazing Grace* (New York: Riverhead Books, 1998) 55.

4. Ibid., 56–57.

5. Wendell Berry, "V," *Given* (Emeryville CA: Shoemaker & Hoard, 2005) 85.

6. Leviticus 26:26.

7. Psalm 17:15 and Psalm 145:16, NRSV.

8. See Matthew 14:20; 15:37; Mark 6:42; 8:8; and Luke 9:17.

9. Norris, *Amazing Grace*, 56–57.

10. Frederick Buechner, *Wishful Thinking: A Theological ABC* (New York: Harper & Row, 1973) 69.

11. 1 Timothy 6:6, NRSV.

12. 1 Timothy 6:6, *The Message*.

Chapter 14

The Posture of Peacemaking

> I refuse to accept the idea that the "is-ness" of man's present nature makes him morally incapable of reaching up for the eternal "ought-ness" that forever confronts him.
> —Martin Luther King Jr.[1]

My husband and I have a plan to save money so we can retire someday. I'm not sure what his vision of retirement entails, but mine includes a house with a big porch where I can sit and drink coffee in the morning, looking out over moving water. I think about inviting people to long, leisurely dinners with us on that porch, like children, grandchildren, and longtime friends. I picture us sitting and talking, watching the sunset reflect on the water.

Right now, when we have people over, we all scramble around the table, adjusting high chairs and boosters, cutting food into child-sized bites, and then later making peanut butter and jelly sandwiches if the meal didn't go over so well. Then we usually find ourselves standing around in the back yard together looking out over the scenic slip-and-slide and our goofy, grass-covered kids. These are good times, too, and someday I know I'll look back and long for them. Every now and then, however, when I'm tired, I'd like to trade just one day of this rambunctious phase of life with the calm serenity we're saving money to enjoy. The good life. Finally, some peace.

Recently, however, I've had to redefine my understanding of peace. Every time I used to read this word, either in the Bible or on a bumper sticker somewhere, I assumed it meant the absence of conflict. Instead, I'm finding that peace has less to do with inactivity and more to do with wholeness, fullness, and a sense of "intended-ness." The Hebrew word *shalom* conveys these ideas, speaking more to a sense of well-being and wholeness than the lack of tension or problems. Frederick Buechner says, "In Hebrew peace, *shalom*, means fullness, means having everything you need to be wholly and happily yourself . . . . For Jesus, peace seems to have meant not the absence of struggle, but the presence of love."[2] According to these definitions, peace isn't experienced when nothing is going on; rather, peace comes in the process of living life, with all its struggles.

This means I shouldn't long for inactivity, but that I am now able, if I choose, to feel a sense of calm intention and rest as I go throughout my day, no matter the circumstances. This means the Bible talks about the ability to have the sitting-out-on-the-porch peace in the midst of toddler time. This definition of peace is so much broader and more revolutionary, giving me the ability to recognize the fullness of a moment. It also requires much more of me because, instead of being a victim of my circumstances, I must opt for love in the midst of chaos. "The 'peace' the gospel brings," says Walter Wink, "is never the absence of conflict, but an ineffable divine reassurance within the heart of conflict: a peace that surpasses understanding."[3] We feel God's peace not when we sit on the beach under an umbrella sipping a cool drink, but when we lovingly live out the wholeness and intentionality he's brought to our lives.

This requires action. It requires us to realize that God's goal is not to orchestrate the tranquility of our lives, but rather to work toward the loving rightness and wholeness of the world. It requires us to stop longing for our conflict-free lives but rather pray "thy kingdom come" in the midst of life's clashes. It means peace is work.

We must practice the posture of peacemaking. We're used to struggling for peace, but sometimes that struggle looks like personal attempts to realize individual goals of the tranquil, front-porch life. Instead of feeling sorry for ourselves when our lives and schedules aren't free of conflict, what if we focused our efforts on loving others in the midst of the conflicts? Maybe we should ask ourselves whether we struggle for the peace that matters. Are we recognizing and grieving over the things in our world that would grieve God? Are we looking to right the wrongs we see, or are we not even looking around?

Bill Cosby delivers a hilarious sketch about how parents, hearing a sibling argument from another room, usually swoop in and try to end the conflict in the quickest way possible, sometimes even before finding out the reason for the fuss. "Parents," he says, "aren't interested in justice. They want *quiet!*"[4]

I wonder if non-Christians think that's the motto Christ-followers have adopted. Do we choose tranquility over justice? Are we content when we shouldn't be? In his book *Holy Discontent*, author and pastor Bill Hybels writes, "If you're not careful, you will become lulled into a state of satisfaction, safety, and serenity, and you'll altogether neglect needs in the world that should elicit *deep discontent* when you see them going unmet."[5] He speaks of Christians needing to live with a holy discontent, a "constant awareness that what is wrecking them is wrecking the heart of God."[6] We must be willing to practice peacemaking, to step outside our quest for the good life and align ourselves with the right-making action of God, even if it means we jeopardize our own tranquility. As Wink writes, "The work of Christ involves radical critique of society."[7]

One of my favorite poems, "Peace" by Gerard Manley Hopkins, deals with this subject.

> When will you ever, Peace, wild wooddove, shy wings shut,
> Your round me roaming end, and under be my boughs?
> When, when, Peace, will you, Peace? I'll not play hypocrite
> To own my heart: I yield you do come sometimes; but
> That piecemeal peace is poor peace. What pure peace allows
> Alarms of wars, the daunting wars, the death of it?
>
> O surely, reaving Peace, my Lord should leave in lieu
> Some good! And so he does leave Patience exquisite,
> That plumes to Peace thereafter. And when Peace here does house
> He comes with work to do, he does not come to coo,
> He comes to brood and sit.[8]

Did you catch the last three lines? Only in recognizing that peace comes with work to do can we realize the whole, full life Christ intends for his followers.

Sometimes it's hard even to know where to start our peacemaking. Where should we be content, and where should we let our discontent lead us to work for the common good? Lately, my daughter, Lucy, has asked me odd questions out of the blue. The other morning, she asked, "Are fruit snacks a sweet or just food?" I later realized she was asking me this because she knew when she could have food and when she got to have a sweet, and she was trying to fit fruit snacks into that framework. Another time, as I fixed her hair in front of the mirror, she asked, "Mommy, is this a sad face or a happy one?" We spent the next few minutes making funny faces in the mirror and assigning them to all sorts of emotions so that she could begin to understand people.

To me, these seem like funny questions, but I realize that Lucy doesn't know where everything fits yet in this Big People world, and she needs me to help her. In the same way, I've recognized in my own life a need to ask God to show me the areas where I should be content and the issues where he wants me to work for peace. I don't know where everything fits in this new, kingdom framework, so I must simply go to him. Imagine how much better prioritized my calendar would be if I began every day asking God to show me where I should be content and where I should spend time working to make things better.

How would our days—and our world—be better prioritized if we all asked, "Lord, where should I be content? What should cause me discontent?" Are there struggles in our lives we should let go and others we need to embrace? Are there situations where we should tell ourselves, "I'm okay with this," and others where we need to ask, "How can I be okay with that?" What would our communities look like if our churches prayed as a body for God to teach us where we should be content and where we should get busy working? Before we assume we know the rules and begin haphazard attempts at peace, let's ask the Prince of Peace to teach us.

Another way of looking at peacemaking is that we should be willing to act in order to extend our peace in Christ. In chapter 6 of a letter he wrote to the Ephesians, Paul says our feet should be fitted with the readiness that comes from the gospel of peace. This active image is about readiness. We should be moved to action by the divine reassurance, making sure that such love is available to others in the midst of their conflicts. "Our goal," says Walter Wink, "must be the training of millions of nonviolent activists who are ready, at a moment's notice, to swing into action on behalf of the humanizing purposes of God."[9]

In this way, we are a sent people. The posture of peacemaking is not just a personal one, nor is it one for those with fair-weather faith. The image of the shoes Paul uses suggests readiness for a long march, and it is a march we need to take together. The prophet Isaiah foresaw this march when he wrote, "How beautiful upon the mountains are the feet of the messenger who announces peace, who brings good news, who announces salvation."[10]

Additionally, we need to pay attention to the methods we use to bring about rightness and justice. How we make peace is just as important as the end we have in mind. It says volumes to others about who our God is and how he works in the world. I can't tell you how many hateful letters I've received from "Christian" organizations lobbying against homosexuality, or hate-filled e-mails about political candidates or people of other religions who don't happen to celebrate Christmas. When will we realize that using hatred as motivation is not the way to communicate our God to others? When will we stop using the world's tools to rally ourselves and instead choose love, the tool Christ used?

Author and scholar Chris Marshall says Jesus was always aware of the means he used as well as the end he was bringing about. "To fight for the kingdom with the weapons of the enemy was to lose the kingdom by default. To fight for the kingdom by turning the other cheek, going the second mile, praying for one's persecutors, loving one's enemies, was to achieve true victory over satanic evil. It was a revolutionary way of being revoluntionary."[11] In his book *The Powers that Be*, Walter Wink, whom I quoted earlier, talks about not becoming what we hate when working against injustices in the world: "When we resist evil with evil, when we lash out at it in kind, we simply guarantee its perpetuation, as we ourselves are made over into its likeness. The way of nonviolence, the way Jesus chose, is the only way that is able to overcome evil without creating new forms of evil and making us evil in return."[12] He writes about finding a third way, not cowering to injustices in the world but not giving in to their methods or ideologies either. "In Jesus' third way," Wink says, "the means we employ must be commensurate with the new order we desire."[13]

We also need to guard against allowing our discontent to be divisive. If we work to be peacemakers, we need to do so both *within and outside* the church body. This requires patience and love from those within the body of Christ, from those who observe someone else's holy discontent, and from those who can't understand why everyone else doesn't jump on board with their peacemaking projects. Many times, a spirit of disunity can frustrate the most noble of pursuits.

How can we guard against this? We need to use extra patience and love when another person expresses discontent about an issue either within or outside the church. We need not be quick to call that person contentious, but rather to recognize how the person needs to be heard and loved. We must recognize the image of God within that person and the issues that are important to him or her, realizing that the person is probably not trying to make others feel bad, but trying to move others to action in this area of holy discontent.

The other side of this issue is the necessity of patience and love with people who might not feel the same level of holy discontent that you feel about a problem. We need to avoid being territorial about our "discontentment" pursuits, recognizing that not everyone shares our love for a particular cause or issue. Instead of thinking those who don't share your passions are not "real Christians," recognize the beauty of diversity within the body of Christ. Instead of being angry with others for not feeling your urgency about an issue, give them grace and time to come around. Who knows? The Lord might move the person you thought would never get on board to lead the next issue you need to tackle.

There is amazing diversity and equality within the body of Christ. If we were all the same, it wouldn't work. If we all had the same passions and causes and discontentment, it wouldn't work. In 1 Corinthians 12:4-8, Paul talks about the way the diverse-but-equal three persons of the Trinity motivate us to different kinds of undertakings: "Now there are varieties of gifts, but the same Spirit; and there are varieties of services, but the same Lord; and there are varieties of activities, but it is the same God who activates all of them in everyone. To each is given the manifestation of the Spirit for the common good."

In this way, we need to continue our journey of peacemaking: in patience and in love, not with self-pity but with courage, not with a quick burst of energy but with steady, persistent strength. We must long not for inactivity, but for loving intentionality.

A friend who lived in Turkey for a time told us that, although he ran a business, his main role was that of a peacemaker. Because of the legacy of the Crusades and the current understanding of Christians that most Turks had, he felt that his intention each day was to make peace, whether by chatting with local businessmen or by being a good husband and dad.

I guess I need to rework my retirement daydreams. Maybe instead of that waterfront porch and the long, lazy meal, I should envision another lively dinner table at a children's home somewhere in Africa. Lord, what would you have? Where would you have me making peace?

Practicing the Postures

1. What is your definition of peace? Pray and ask God to give you his understanding.
2. Where in your life are you making peace? Are there areas in your life that grieve you and that grieve the heart of God? Pray about what you are doing or what God might lead you to do.

Notes

1. Quoted in Bill Hybels, *Holy Discontent* (Grand Rapids: Zondervan, 1997) 33.

2. Frederick Buechner, *Wishful Thinking: A Theological ABC* (New York: Harper & Row, 1973) 69.

3. Walter Wink, *The Powers that Be* (New York: Doubleday, 1998) 121.

4. *Bill Cosby Himself,* DVD, dir. Bill Cosby, Twentieth Century Fox, 1982.

5. Hybels, *Holy Discontent,* 29.

6. Ibid., 27.

7. Wink, *The Powers that Be,* 90.

8. Gerard Manley Hopkins, "Peace," in *The One Year Book of Poetry,* Philip Comfort and Daniel Partner, eds. (Wheaton IL: Tyndale House, 1999) June 29.

9. Wink, *The Powers that Be,* 121.

10. Isaiah 52:7, NRSV.

11. Chris Marshall, "A Prophet of God's Justice: Reclaiming the Political Jesus," *Stimulus* 14/3 (August 2006): 39.

12. Wink, *The Powers that Be,* 127.

13. Ibid., 113.

Chapter 15

The Posture of Sharing

When God's kingdom comes in its fullness, poverty and pain will be no more. In the meantime, God's kingly power is at work in Jesus and his followers to bring healing and liberation and to create a new community to work against poverty, hunger and misery.

—Chris Marshall[1]

My preschool-aged daughter and I have exchanged four-letter words recently. She loves to use a particular word, and when I hear it come out of her mouth, it feels as though someone is sticking pins underneath my fingernails. I know I'm not the only parent whose child has a problem with this four-letter word, but some days I feel that I am. Immediately, I think, "Does she say this word in front of other people when I'm not around? What will her Sunday school teachers think?" Then I reel with waking nightmares of the other ministers at church having to pull my husband aside and talk to him about his daughter's use of this word in the House of God. Usually, my fear motivates me to combat my daughter's language issues with a four-letter word of my own, and then the game begins: we exchange our words back and forth until one of us blinks. I am determined to win this battle, so I don't blink. I don't know where the line between consistent parenting and qualifying for the nuthouse is drawn, but many times, this line seems fuzzy to me.

Lucy's word? "Mine." I *hate* the sound of this word. We tried hard not to use it around her, and yet, it seems to have arisen from the depths of her soul. When she first began talking, this was one of her most repeated words; while we struggled to understand her simplest words like "milk" or "truck" or "cookie," one "mine!" from her reverberated through the length of our house at least ten times. So, rational parent that I was, I decided to combat this four-letter word with one of my own: "ours." Surely I could impart a love and value for other human beings simply by offering her another way to look at life. As those of you with children know, rational parenting is like the Loch Ness Monster. We all hope it's out there somewhere, but we don't know anyone who has actually discovered it (and if we do come across someone who claims to have found it, deep down we think that person is a little off).

My family decided to step the battle up a notch. We loaded the iPod with several of Jack Johnson's brilliant sing-a-longs containing lyrics like, "It's always more fun to share with everyone" and "If you have two, give one to your friend." My husband and I have enjoyed this music because, unlike most children's music, it doesn't drive us crazy. It could be because it has acoustic guitar and piano instead of the typical "music box" accompaniment, or it could be that we've discovered there are only so many times you can catch yourself singing "Elmo's World" before your own gag reflex kicks in.

While grooving to words like "If you have one, here is something you can learn: you can still share, just by taking turns," I began to think. Why is "The Sharing Song" considered a children's song? Adults need to hear this message just as much as children do, and maybe more. After all, if I'm not willing to give up my morning latte in protest of certain coffee companies that demean their overseas workers, can I discipline Lucy because she tries to take a plastic teacup from another toddler? I began to think maybe our children don't merely hear the word "mine" and begin saying it; maybe they see the word out loud in our behavior.

This kind of selfishness is likely a two-part problem, stemming from both human nature and environment, as do many of our "issues." Apart from Christ, humans are not living out the fullness of God's intention for humanity. We need Jesus to teach us what our attitudes should be as members not only of this planet, but also of the kingdom of God. We need to practice a posture of sharing.

If we look at the Bible, we discover much biblical evidence to support this posture in the Old Testament, in Jesus' ministry on earth, and in the life of the New Testament church. These examples don't tell us to share just so others can identify us as Christians due to our good behavior. They tell us that God's people are supposed to live in a communal nature, seeking to benefit others out of reverence for him.

In the Old Testament, Amos speaks of Israel's unwillingness to maintain social justice because of its lavish lifestyle. He criticizes those who live in luxury at the expense of the poor in his day, holding that *how* God's people gain wealth and *what* they do with it clearly matter to God. Consistently, the book of Amos (especially 5:21-24) and the rest of the prophetic literature hold that Yahweh will intervene because of the mistreatment of the helpless. Additionally, it is important to note that the prophetic materials are rooted in the communal nature of the law; it is not enough to consider only one's own plight.

In a similar manner, Jesus addresses the posture of sharing our resources more than any other social issue. His proclamation to his hometown in Luke 4 is full of jubilee language that speaks of revolution (letting the land rest for a year and transferring it back to its original owner, etc.; see God's command for jubilee in Leviticus 25 and 27). Unfortunately, the people of Nazareth, and the people of Israel for that matter, merely tightened their grip on their possessions. They were unwilling to commit to the upheaval caused by the jubilee. Jesus preached, nonetheless, about a spirit of selflessness that would radically reorient society under the kingdom of God.

In Acts 2:44-47, Luke tells us about the first church's posture of sharing and how it demonstrated the lifestyle demanded by the kingdom Jesus brought. Notice that the placement of the phrase "And day by day the Lord added to their number those who were being saved" is vital; Luke is clearly saying that the early church's lifestyle gave credibility and power to its witness. Acts 4:32–5:11 illustrates this further. A positive example of selfless sharing is evident in Barnabas; immediately following his story, we find a negative example in the lives of Ananias and Sapphira.

Scripture as a whole, then, provides ample evidence for the posture of sharing. It reminds us that, though difficult, we must be willing to live our lives respective of others in the world. Walter Harrelson, professor of Old Testament at Vanderbilt University, strongly states, "Overeating and over-consumption, gross inequity in the control of wealth, and *a desire to maintain one's own style of life irrespective of world family* clearly constitutes sin in the biblical perspective."[2] If we are concerned only with our personal well-being and let the well-being of others slide into the background, we sin; we chip away at the true humanity Jesus paid the ultimate price to restore in us. Richard Baer agrees: "Should we in America refuse to alter our lifestyle, I believe we will experience increasing dehumanization—of ourselves—both individually and corporately. To begin to share on a broad scale, therefore, is not just a matter of obedience to God or of altruism but rather a necessary requirement for remaining human."[3]

My friends in the Baylor Chemistry Department helped me flesh out this idea. Imagine yourself in a chemistry lab, placing a glass test tube over a Bunsen burner. In the test tube is a solution of salt water, a homogenous mixture of table salt and water. Your goal is to ensure that the mixture in the test tube stays in solution, meaning you must maintain equal amounts of salt and water. What happens if you turn on the Bunsen burner underneath the test tube? After a while, the water in the test tube begins to evaporate, leaving you with plain salt. In order to keep a solution of salt and water under these new conditions, you must take a dropper full of water and vigilantly drop corresponding amounts of water into the test tube. You have to be attentive, regularly adding water to your test tube, or else you quickly end up with something other than the solution you intended.

Americans live in the top percentage of the world in terms of wealth, education, and opportunity. We also live in a consumer-based system that tells us it can provide our every fantasy—for a price. We can no longer assume that we can maintain the state of humanity God intended for us. The conditions in which we live require that we become vigilant, attentively seeking Christ to renew our humanity. We must ask him to help us, to reveal to us the ever-present opportunities to share with others. In this way, we counteract the flames of selfishness that alter our humanity. If we are disciplined and consistently practice the posture of sharing, drop after drop, Christ graces our lives with the kingdom humanity he died for us to know.

John Woolman, an abolitionist and member of the Society of Friends who lived in America during the 1700s, can help us get started. For Woolman, true faith was a "both-and" situation; both an inward state of devotion to the Creator-God and an outward awareness and administration of his justice are necessary to live in accordance with the truth of God's kingdom. This balance is difficult to maintain, isn't it? Woolman issued a challenge to those who had come to the New World for personal wealth and gain: live with a communal understanding of the creation of God.

> . . . a belief was gradually settled in my mind that if such who had great estates generally lived in that humility and plainness which belongs to the Christian life, and laid much easier rents and interests on their lands and moneys and thus led the way to a right use of things, so great a number of people might be employed in things useful that labour both for men and other creatures would need to be no more than an agreeable employ, and divers branches of business which serves chiefly to please the natural inclinations of our minds might in the way of pure wisdom be discontinued.[4]

This thought was challenging then, and it challenges us now. Can—and *will*—people see the value of God's creation enough to change their singular lifestyles for the benefit of the whole? Woolman's understanding of true religion demanded nothing less. To this end, Woolman stopped wearing dyed clothing, using silver vessels, and (at times) traveling any other way than on foot. These he saw not only as resignation unto God, but also as instructors in empathy. "I was not only taught patience but also made thankful to God, who thus led me about and instructed me that I might have a quick and lively feeling of the afflictions of my fellow creatures whose situation in life is difficult."[5] Woolman summarized his views on outward and inward religion with this striking thought: "Our gracious Creator cares and provides for all his creatures. His tender mercies are over all his works; and so far as his love influences our minds, so far we become interested in his workmanship and feel a desire to take hold of every opportunity to lessen the distresses of the afflicted and increase the happiness of the creation."[6] Our goal, said Woolman, should be to be so grounded in the love we receive from the divine that we do all we can to increase not our own happiness, but that of those around us.

Ironically, two hundred years later (1974), the International Congress on World Evangelism in Lausanne came to the same conclusion: "All of us are shocked by the poverty of millions and disturbed by the injustices which cause it. Those of us who live in affluent circumstances accept our duty to develop a simple life-style in order to contribute more generously to both relief and evangelism."[7] Many see the resistance to this kind of lifestyle founded in early economic thought. Adam Smith's *Wealth of Nations* speaks to the false idea that "the good of the whole was insured if all people would pursue their own self-interest."[8] Mennonite author Arthur Gish reminds us, "There cannot be justice for all as long as anyone consumes more than one needs . . . . Overconsumption is theft. We privileged people are the major source of the world's problems and they will not be solved before we give up our privileged position."[9] Author Adam Daniel Finnerty makes a stark comment on our unwillingness to adapt a posture of sharing as well: "If we are not able to forge a society that feeds the hungry and clothes the naked, it will not be because the resources aren't there. It will be because people were unwilling to let themselves hope and lacked the courage to take the risk."[10]

"Okay," you say. "I am convinced of the importance of global sharing and a communal outlook. But getting started is overwhelming." You've encountered another obstacle in this posture: the task quickly gets complex.

With good intentions, you begin to dig into these ideas and are suddenly hit with fair trade issues, shrinking life expectancy rates for those in Africa, and figures of how much money is spent on arms annually across the globe. Argh! We need handles by which we can begin to take hold of these selfish monstrosities and do our part to carry our load.

Luckily, John Woolman gives us tools by which we can begin to examine our lives and willingness to share. First, he says we should be acquainted with the labor and hardships of others, physical or otherwise. This fosters what he calls a "tenderness of heart" toward other people. Second, Woolman says we should ask ourselves questions such as:

Does my budget take care of others as well as myself and my own family?

Do I buy certain things with my money because other people buy those same things?

Do I take the chances I'm given to lessen others' hardships, giving them a better chance to enjoy life?[11]

After aligning some of these inner aspects of the posture of sharing, author Richard Foster gives several practical suggestions that further provide active steps we can take to align ourselves outwardly:

Buy things for their usefulness rather than their status.

Reject anything that is producing an addiction in you. (Refuse to be a slave to anything but God.)

Develop a habit of giving things away.

Refuse to be propagandized by the custodians of modern gadgetry. (Often "new" features seduce us into buying what we do not need.)

Learn to enjoy things without owning them.

Develop a deeper appreciation for the creation.

Look with a healthy skepticism at all "buy now, pay later" schemes.

Obey Jesus' instructions about plain, honest speech.

Reject anything that breeds the oppression of others.

Shun anything that distracts you from seeking first the kingdom of God.[12]

So, until Lucy and I can discuss these things together, I need to model the posture of sharing in front of her. After all, when Jack Johnson sings, "If you've got one sandwich, cut that thing in half," it quietly echoes of Proverbs 1:19. "When you grab all you can get, that's what happens: the more you get, the less you are."

Practicing the Postures

1. This week, begin asking yourself Woolman's three questions when you are faced with purchasing and budgetary decisions.
2. Pray through Richard Foster's list of suggestions on simplicity and see what God leads you to do.

Notes

1. Chris Marshall, "A Prophet of God's Justice: Reclaiming the Political Jesus," *Stimulus* 14/3 (August 2006): 36.

2. Harrelson, quoted in Richard J. Foster, *Freedom of Simplicity* (San Francisco: Harper&Row, 1981) 148, italics mine.

3. Baer, quoted in Adam Daniel Finnerty, *No More Plastic Jesus: Global Justice and Christian Lifestyle* (Maryknoll NY: Orbis Books, 1977) 167.

4. Moulton Phillips, ed., *The Journal and Major Essays of John Woolman* (Richmond IN: Friends United Press, 1971) 118–19.

5. Ibid., 137.

6. Ibid., 241.

7. Richard J. Foster, *Freedom of Simplicity* (San Francisco: Harper&Row, 1981) 128.

8. Smith, quoted in Richard J. Foster, *Freedom of Simplicity* (San Francisco: Harper&Row, 1981) 174.

9. Gish, quoted in Finnerty, *No More Plastic Jesus*, 167.

10. Finnerty, *No More Plastic Jesus*, 167.

11. Information in this paragraph is paraphrased from Phillips, ed., *The Journal and Major Essays of John Woolman*, 241–42.

12. Richard J. Foster, *Celebration of Discipline: The Path to Spiritual Growth*, rev. ed. (San Francisco: HarperCollins, 1988) 90–95.

Chapter 16

The Posture of Tolerance

Judgment immobilizes, only hopeful love leaves an opening for God's alternative future.

—Jürgen Moltmann[1]

Remember the childhood game Red Rover? Remember lining up in your elementary school gym, neighborhood park, or backyard with a bunch of other children, then standing in two opposing lines with hands clasped together? At the chorus, "Red Rover, Red Rover, send _____ right over," the named child careened from one line toward the other line in search of a weak spot through which to burst. If he ran through the tightly clasped hands, he got to pick a person from the other line to take back with him to his line. If he did not make it through, he was made to join the enemy line.

I would like to say that my participation in this simple game was a lovely pastime enjoyed by sweet children. However, I think there's probably a reason this game is no longer the sportsmanship game of choice for P.E. programs. Alas, the opportunity to flatten some of the kids who bugged you the most seemed to motivate this game. I am not proud to admit that many times, my line deliberately called the name of the mousiest, frailest subject and then bound our arms together so tightly that we even forgot the boy-girl cootie issue in an effort to create an impenetrable chain. Most games in which I was involved never finished before someone was knocked flat on his back so badly he went sobbing in agony to the nearest adult.

I bring up these memories not to pour on the guilt if you were one of the bullies, nor to send you back to your therapist if you were one of the kids who repeatedly got creamed. I bring up these memories because I fear that, many times, the church and followers of Jesus continue playing this game of Red Rover as they interact with society. We seem to have lost the ability to interact with others who do not share our beliefs or values. Many times we act as though the lines are drawn, and one must burst through another's line in order to claim victory. But should this be the nature of the interaction between those who call themselves believers and those who do not? If we call ourselves participants in the kingdom of God, we do not have the ability to disengage from the lives of others; we must develop a posture of tolerance.

It is easy to surround yourself with people who think in the same ways, believe the same ideas, and live life in similar patterns. Many communities are made up of the same kind of people to the extent that we intentionally have to seek people whose stories are completely different from ours. It is comfortable to go through a week and interact only with those who are like us. People like us are usually where we are. People with values similar to ours are probably at the same places we find ourselves. People who think what we think usually go to the same restaurants, churches, and grocery stores that we frequent.

Why is it, then, that we should venture beyond the familiar? Is homogeneity such a problem for individuals who follow Christ? After all, it is hard work to be in relationship with those who are different from us. Many times, it is exhausting to try to understand each other or to come to any kind of common ground. It is certainly more comfortable for us to interact with what is familiar. However, it isn't how we gain a wide understanding of the people in our world or build deep, honest relationships with others. It isn't how we engage reality or become skilled at loving people. It isn't how we learn.

If we consistently remain around those like us, we assume that the whole world views life our way. We are surprised and resentful when someone misunderstands us or when a friend does something we don't understand. We begin to use phrases like "the *right* way to think" and "the *wrong* kind of people." We begin to demonize those who choose differently before we even try to understand the context in which they made the choices. Soon, the colonial language that taught us to say "the *wrong* side of the road" instead of "the opposite side of the road" begins to color our language. The more we surround ourselves with other versions of ourselves, the more we become convinced of our own rightness. The more we seek homogeneity, the more closed off we become to other ideas and, what's worse, to other *people*. If we live only in our own circle of "right ideas" and "right people," we begin to miss others' lives altogether. We as the church must realize that there are millions of people in this world (indeed, within the Christian faith) who do not live by our worldview, and we must learn how to interact with them, love them, and *tolerate* them.

Many of us who follow Christ need to reclaim the word "tolerance" and ensure that it doesn't take on a meaning akin to "putting up with those who disagree with you." We should guard the word and the way we use it so that it does not begin to adopt the meaning of universalism, of "anything goes" in the realm of faith. Tolerance means we acknowledge others' views even though we don't adhere to them. What is more, tolerance should mean we begin to acknowledge others' *lives*, an act that made Jesus' ministry so revolutionary.

One of the definitions of *respect* in Webster's Dictionary is "courteous expressions of regard: now chiefly in *pay one's respects* to show polite regard by visiting or presenting oneself."[2] While we tend to think of paying one's respects as something we do upon a person's death, is this idea not an interesting one as it relates to a discussion of tolerance and respect? Shouldn't we as Christ-followers begin to link the idea of tolerance with the image of paying respects? What if we began to think of tolerance as showing courteous expressions of regard, as visiting another or presenting oneself? What if we began to incarnate the grace and truth in which we so passionately believe? What if we saw differences in culture, in moral choices, and in belief as reasons to *engage* people instead of excuses to disengage and quickly exit? What if we entered into dialogue with others and invited others to the game instead of taking our ball and going home? What if we, still being our Christ-following selves, began to acknowledge and love the lives of others, whether or not we approved of how they live them? What difference would that make in the ways we interact with those in our daily lives with whom we differ?

If we look at the Bible, we see that this kind of tolerance, acknowledging the lives of others, is not a hypothetical scenario for our own day. It is a behavior required of all who call themselves followers of Christ, in the biblical account up to the present day, if only because we see Jesus modeling it.

Did not Christ display this kind of respect, this love for others, by presenting himself to the world? Think of the woman at the well in John 4. Jesus pays his respects to a woman who not only was an outcast from her own society (because of her marital history) but who was also an outcast from his (as he was a Jew and she was a Samaritan). Jesus engages her in dialogue on issues of true worship, and his courteous expressions reveal to her that he is the Messiah. Christ reveals the way to acknowledge the lives of others and demonstrates his willingness to "show up," purposefully traveling through Samaria when his disciples want to avoid it.

The Bible shows us repeatedly that Jesus liked dialogue, and he was good at engaging others. He spent time approaching heart issues with people such as Nicodemus, the Pharisees, Mary, Martha, Matthew and his tax collector friends, Zacchaeus, and others. We could delve into the mysteries of his reasoning or study these characters each in depth. For now, it is enough to note that this behavior of his, this habit of paying his respects and presenting himself to others, is not something he did simply "because he's Jesus." It is one that we, as his followers, should strive to emulate. We must note the way he extended courteous expressions of regard to people of different cultures and moral practices. We must practice tolerance as he did.

We can also look at the life of Paul, who strove to practice Christ's behavior and teachings. Paul engaged all kinds of lives in his ministry. How many times in Acts do we read of him entering synagogues, amphitheatres, or other public places in order to encounter others? He did not merely walk in with tracts, preach a prepared sermon, and watch as people signed up for a "life in Christ." Instead, he took questions, he spoke, he listened, and he lived alongside people. Paul also speaks in 1 Corinthians 9 about his willingness to live life with people of all cultures and to give himself up for them.

It is important to note that, in the lives of Jesus and Paul, we find two people who were not in any way apologetic about their beliefs or about the fact that they were different from those with whom they lived life. In their lives, and in our own, tolerance and respect for others does not place one in a bland meaninglessness of belief. Rather, tolerance allowed them and allows us to taste the honest wholeness of humanity in a way that is full of depth, honor, and truth.

In this manner, the expanded idea of tolerance keeps us from damaging our message and the One who sends it by the way we impart it. We must learn to be agreeable with those with whom we completely disagree. In his book *Sermon on the Mount,* Clarence Jordan adeptly writes, "People who are right are usually in the greatest danger of becoming a nuisance. The fact that they are right, and know it, has a powerful tendency to make them intolerant of those who are not in a position to see it their way. And this further alienates the very people who need to be drawn closer. Truth, thus, is hurt by its own advocates."[3]

One of the most important lessons we learn from a study of tolerance is the need to ensure we are continually in relationship with those who are unlike us. Many Western Christians fail to be in relationship with those outside their belief systems, and this is contrary to what we see in the life of Christ. We should welcome others and feel welcomed by them to explore life together in a meaningful way. If we know others outside our own circle of belief, it's a good start. But how *well* do we know them? Many times we work with, play soccer with, and socialize with others only to fall silent around the "real" issues, which is also contrary to the life of Christ. Craig Blomberg makes an accurate yet troubling assessment of these matters, saying, "Many Christians barely know any non-Christians well enough to share their faith in less than superficial fashion."[4]

"Aha!" you might say to yourself if you are a good evangelical. "We are finally getting to the point: sharing your faith with others." What you might have wondered all along is whether or not this "tolerance speak" has a purpose, or if we are simply rearguing a new form of universalism, something like, "Let's come together, dialogue about our own faiths over a cup of coffee, and then go away, each exactly the same as before." This is not the point, although there is a necessary element of change involved in a dialogue of this kind. We must consider, however, that the change may take place in our own lives, as each interaction with others on matters of faith has something to teach us. Our responsibility lies in our willingness to journey in faith and share our faith stories with others at every opportunity. Further, we have need for a new understanding of tolerance because we are responsible for the *manner* in which we share such stories. We are not responsible for the change itself, either that in others or in ourselves. All we can do is intentionally dedicate ourselves to the dialogue and pray that grace intervenes on each side.

Usually discussions of tolerance devolve into a delineation of the ways in which *others* need to change so we (the ones who feel we're in the right) do not have to tolerate them anymore. If we practice the art of noticing, however, and do so introspectively, we find that the practice of tolerance is one that requires change in the only person you can control: yourself. The responsibility of the posture of tolerance lies with the one who has promised to lay down his life for the sake of others, just as his or her Savior has done. It is our choice to make a conscious effort to engage and acknowledge the lives of others; it is the One we follow who is defamed when we don't.

May we follow Christ's example, engaging all people with the same hopeful love in which he envelopes us. May we say to ourselves, "He has access to God, I want to remove the obstacles, as much as I can. God has come to him, he needs to be able to come to God."[5]

Practicing the Postures

1. Pray and ask God about the definition of tolerance, both yours and his.
2. Do you share life in meaningful ways with anyone who is different from you? Do you know anyone from outside your circle of belief? If you have trouble naming these relationships, pray and ask God to expand your circles.

Notes

1. Jürgen Moltmann, "The Hope for the Kingdom of God and Signs of Hope in the World: The Relevance of Blumhardt's Theology Today," *Pneuma: The Journal of the Society for Pentecostal Studies* 26/1 (Spring 2004): 11.

2. *Webster's New World College Dictionary*, 3rd ed., s.v. "respect."

3. Clarence Jordan, *Sermon on the Mount* (Valley Forge: Judson, 1952) 40.

4. Craig Blomberg, *1 Corinthians* (NIV Application Commentary; Grand Rapids: Zondervan, 1995) 188.

5. Jürgen Moltmann, "The Hope for the Kingdom of God and Signs of Hope in the World: The Relevance of Blumhardt's Theology Today," *Pneuma: The Journal of the Society for Pentecostal Studies* 26/1 (Spring 2004): 10.

Chapter 17

Conclusion: The Posture of Love

The believing community in any generation will enter into relationship with Jesus only when it takes on and lives out the love of the incarnation.

—Gail R. O'Day[1]

In just about every yoga class I've attended, there's been a student who asks the instructor, "If I only have five minutes a day to do yoga, what pose should I do?" It's always interesting to sit back and take in the scenario that follows because of the different styles of the teachers and the various motivations of the students.

Sometimes this question comes from a man who wants to compare yoga philosophies with the teacher or quiz the teacher to see if he or she measures up. Sometimes it is asked by a ragged woman whom a doctor sent to class to learn relaxation techniques. Other students ask this question because they're overwhelmed and need a concrete way to dive into the whole yoga thing.

The answers I've heard from the teachers vary as much as the students' motivations. Some teachers who have adjusted their careers, eating preferences, and beliefs to an all-encompassing yogic lifestyle gently try to help the student understand that yoga is not a quick, five-minute-a-day fix, but about the process of developing awareness, which is hard to do in five minutes a day. Other teachers simply make a face that says, "If you're only going to give five minutes a day, don't bother." Still other teachers guide overwhelmed students to one or two postures they already know, giving them a place to begin.

Some poses, learned in the earliest yoga classes, encompass all the health benefits of even the trickiest, most impressive-looking postures. One of these is called Adhomukha Svanasana, or Downward-facing Dog. The practice of this posture is a lifelong process, and even some who've practiced yoga for years have trouble with it. It doesn't come easy for me. I've had fairly tight hamstring muscles all my life, and this pose requires you to put your hands flat on the floor all the while keeping your feet flat on the ground. I can remember some of my first attempts at this pose, straining to get my heels on the ground and listening to my teacher say, "Just relax into the pose." I wondered if I was the only one muttering to myself under my breath when she said, "Do you feel the calming effect of this posture? I could stay here all day. How about you?" *This* is the pose to do if we only have five minutes a day to practice?

Someone asks Jesus, the great teacher, a similar question in Matthew 22:34-40. A young man from an opposing philosophy wanted to test Jesus and asked him which commandment in all of the Jewish law was the most important. Jesus answered him by quoting Deuteronomy 6:5 and Leviticus 19:18 (here in the NRSV): "He said to him, "' You shall love the Lord your God with all your heart, and with all your soul, and with all your mind." This is the greatest and first commandment. And a second is like it: "You shall love your neighbor as yourself." On these two commandments hang all the law and the prophets.'"

The Bible doesn't record the young man's answer. I wonder if he was humbled and silent, recognizing the futility in his attempts to stump the Son of God. Or maybe he just slipped into the crowd, scratching his head. Or, if he was anything like some yoga students I've been around, he might have said, "Love? *Seriously?* That's *it*? Shouldn't it be something more impressive? More advanced? I know I'm supposed to love—I learned that early on. Isn't there something else?"

But some postures, in yoga and in faith, are lifelong journeys. Jesus recognized this, pointing this young man, and us, to the centrality of love. And we, like this young man, have a choice: we can dismiss Jesus' directive to love as quaint, cute, and simplistic, or we can examine why he held it as the central element in a life of faith.

We see in stories about Jesus that *our willingness to assume a posture of love brings about a connection with God that permeates our entire awareness.* As we've seen from Jesus' answer to the young man, love is the most important commandment; it is the chief characteristic of a life related to God. Love, says Jesus, brings about a deep connection with God.

He reminds his disciples of this before his death, something we can read about in John 14 in his Farewell Discourse. Right after he tells his disciples he will not be with them much longer, he says, "Let me give you a new command: Love one another. In the same way I loved you, you love one another. This is how everyone will recognize that you are my disciples—when they see the love you have for each other." The idea that Jesus is leaving distracts the disciples. They question Jesus on the details, missing out on the heart of his teaching: "Love is the chief characteristic in this bond that we have. Your loving actions, your going about love, is what will connect you to each other and to me after I am gone. This loving connection will be so deep that others will see it and see me and my Father because of it."

Jesus tries to return the conversation to these ideas by saying, "The person who knows my commandments and keeps them, that's who loves me. And the person who loves me will be loved by my Father, and *I will love him and make myself plain to him.*" Did you notice those last words? I added italics because, after reading a whole book about developing the art of noticing and practicing faith postures or attitudes, we see that if we're overwhelmed, if we're confused about how to start or need God to make himself plain to us, we can focus on the love we have for God and his love we share with others. We can start there with what Jesus said is the most important commandment, which leads us to a deep understanding of him and an unfathomable relationship with him.

But is what Jesus says conditional? Is he saying he's going to only love those who love him and keep all his rules? One of his disciples, Judas (the Bible says this is not Judas Iscariot but a different Judas), asks him this question next. "Master, why is it that you are about to make yourself plain to us but not to the world?" It's a good question. If Jesus is about to clue the world in on the reality of who he is, why not make sure everyone, the yes-men and the nay-sayers, get the picture? Judas is asking, "Jesus, why don't you want everyone to be able to be with you, to notice you, and to know you?"

"Because a loveless world," says Jesus, "is a sightless world. If anyone loves me, he will carefully keep my word and my Father will love him—we'll move right into the neighborhood!" The limit is not Jesus' love for us, but a limit we place on him. It's not his lack of desire that we know him that separates us, but our blindness to the things of him that hinders our ability to live life deeply with him.

So he tells his disciples and all of us who long for the presence of God in our lives to be about love. It's as if he's saying, "What I've shown you is love. The commands I've given you are about love. If you love me, you'll already be going about these loving things. If you're going about your life doing these loving things, loving fully, as I have, then you'll find yourself in the center of the divine love, aware of the Father's presence with you." Isn't this ultimately what we're about? We, like Jesus' disciples, long for a connection between the human and the divine. We need that deep bond, the relationship that brings about the great reversal, the possibility of hope that springs from despair. And into that need, Jesus speaks, saying, "Remember the root command: Love one another."

This teaching is confirmed in the life of the early church, in the lives of people who did not encounter the physical presence of Jesus while he lived on earth. Not being with him physically didn't hinder their ability to know God or to experience his divine presence. We know this because we read their teachings in the book of 1 John, in chapters 4 and 5:

> Let us continue to love each other since love comes from God. Everyone who loves is born of God and experiences a relationship with God. The person who refuses to love doesn't know the first thing about God, because God *is* love—*so you can't know him if you don't love.* This is how God showed his love for us: God sent his only Son into the world so we might live through him. This is the kind of love we are talking about—not that we once upon a time loved God, but that he loved us and sent his Son as a sacrifice to clear away our sins and the damage they've done to our relationship with God.
>
> My dear, dear friends, if God loved us like this, we certainly ought to love each other. No one has seen God, ever. But *if we love one another, God dwells deeply within us,* and his love becomes complete in us—perfect love! . . . Everyone who confesses that Jesus is God's Son participates continuously in an intimate relationship with God. We know it so well, we've embraced it heart and soul, this love that comes from God.
>
> God is love. *When we take up permanent residence in a life of love, we live in God and God lives in us.* This way, love has the run of the house, becomes at home and mature in us.[2]

If we listen to the teachings of Jesus, and of those who have gone before us, we see that love is the environment in which our understanding of God grows. Love is the place where our connection to him is nurtured at first growth, where it weathers seasons and storms of life, and where it blooms whole and mature. Love enables us to live as his creation. "Abiding in God is not religious fire insurance, which we take out in nervous interest of our self-preservation. Just the opposite: Dwelling in God's love is the habitat for which human beings were originally created and, in Christ, are being re-created."[3] I like how simply this commentator puts it: "Love is what God through Jesus Christ has given the church to know about God and to communicate to others."[4]

We also see from these teachings that a relationship with God isn't about how little I can love and still know God or even what I have to do to be in relationship with him. What we see is *the fullness of God's love abolishes limits on our love for him and others.* Jesus is saying that we ask the wrong question, just as yoga students sometimes want to know how little they can do to receive the benefits of a yogic lifestyle. Jesus is trying to get us to see that love is at the heart of what it means to be in relationship with God, something that permeates our whole outlook, our whole lifestyle, and our whole understanding of self and others. There are no limits to that kind of love because dwelling in God's presence does away with them. Jesus lived a life of this kind of fullness so that we could understand what love really is. He reminds us of this at the end of John 14: "But so the world might know how thoroughly I love the Father, I am carrying out my Father's instructions right down to the last detail."

When you get married, you permanently attach your life to another. It is understood that once you marry, any kind of romantic relationship outside of that with your spouse will cease and any other opportunities for romance will be rejected because of your love for your spouse. Most people don't write these things out before they get married, adding line items for all the things they will stop doing because of their upcoming vows. Why? Because when you get married, you're crazy in love with that other person. You aren't thinking, "What do I have to do or not do?" Instead, you wonder, "What would I *not* do for this person?" You're starting a whole new life, turning everything you've known upside down for the chance to live in relationship with this person who, amazingly, feels the same way about you!

Yes, there are things you do and don't do in a marriage, rules to follow and choices to navigate, just as we all need to practice postures (or rules or commandments about love) to train us toward good. But, if love is the environment in which you live, if you live fully out of your love relationship with your spouse or with God, those choices aren't rules in which you try to find a loophole. Ultimately, it's about a lifestyle of love. As we come to know God, we throw the checklist aside and dwell fully in God's limitless love. "To love one another as Jesus loves us is to live a life thoroughly shaped by a love that knows no limits, by a love whose expression brings the believer closer into relationship with God, with Jesus, and with one another. It is to live a love that carries with it a whole new concept of the possibilities of community."[5]

When my husband and I bought our first house, we moved into a community that had a weekly recycling curbside pick-up. I considered myself enviro-friendly, so I was happy, even proud, to begin putting our aluminum cans out every week next to the trash. I did this for several weeks while we were getting settled. And then, once I was unpacked and settled, a neat thing happened: I read the information the city gave me about all the other materials they would pick up for us, about types of paper, and about the numbering system on the bottom of all plastics. This was an eye opener. All of a sudden, things I'd pitched for years were renewable. I started to ask myself questions. Why couldn't I recycle this milk jug? Do I need all these Ziplock bags? Can't I rinse out the tin cans and the peanut butter containers? Do we need to use paper napkins, or can I use fabric ones? No one made me change, but I noticed all the ways in which I could easily live a greener life. Maybe I was dense before, but all of a sudden, I saw the aluminum can experience spill over into all areas of my life.

Dwelling in God's love is like that: you receive love and see more and more instances where you think, Why shouldn't God's love matter here? Why can't God's love spill over into this situation? How could God's love *not* change this person's life? When you become aware of God's love, it's not about doing the minimum; it's about stripping away all the limitations we put on love and letting God's love loose in all the relationships and situations of our lives.

The earliest Jesus followers saw this connection, how God's love overflows and runs out into our relationships, even with the most difficult of people. Verses from 1 John say, "We, though, are going to love—love and be loved. First we were loved, now we love. He loved us first. If anyone boasts, 'I love God,' and goes right on hating his brother or sister, thinking nothing of it, he is a liar. If he won't love the person he can see, how can he love the God he can't see? The command we have from Christ is blunt: Loving God includes loving people. You've got to love both" (1 John 4:19-21).

Sure, you say. I can do that because this passage speaks to churches of like-minded people, right? Not so, says C. Clifton Black in his commentary on 1, 2, and 3 John:

> Most churches in the first century were not homogeneous associations for the religiously like-minded, having access to the myriad support systems of modern Western society. As Paul, James, and John remind us, the member-

ship of early Christian communities was remarkably diverse, prone to factions, yet heavily dependent on one another for the fulfillment of basic needs. For the members of such churches to assume such familial responsibilities for one another entailed considerable commitment.

It still does. As anyone knows from experience with the wear and tear of real-life Christian community, to regard one's neighbors within the church as Christ's sisters and brothers, and to respond to them as God's children, is scarcely soft and rarely easy. In some churches, just as in some families, it can be much easier to love the homeless and the stranger, those with whom we have brief encounters, than to love those whom we know well and have promised to uphold over the long haul.[6]

Earlier, in the book of 1 John, we read, "For this is the original message we heard: We should love each other. The way we know we've been transferred from death to life is that we love our brothers and sisters . . . . If you see some brother or sister in need and have the means to do something about it but turn a cold shoulder and do nothing, what happens to God's love? It disappears. And you made it disappear" (vv. 11, 14, 17). For this reason, one scholar of the book of 1 John writes poignantly, "We do not interpret 1 John. It interprets us."[7]

These love passages also point to *God's ability to come alongside our acts of love and complete them, perfect them, and make them whole.* We may worry about the effects of our love and then limit our offering based on our fears. We may think our love is of no consequence to someone and stop short. God might put something on our hearts, but we rationalize it away with insecure self-talk. These hesitations are limits we place on the love of God, boundaries to which Jesus never gave a second thought. He boldly announced God's love and desire to set things right on earth, to be in loving relationship with people.

I realize I do this often. On a recent holiday, Lucy and I made cookies to take to our neighbors. We spent the morning making them, letting them cool, wrapping them, and attaching little notes to each bundle to let all the people whose yards touch ours know we are thankful for them. Then, as we walked to each house, I explained to Lucy that we were going to each house that bordered ours. After we delivered the last one, she pointed to a house with which we share about two feet of fence and asked, "Why didn't we take any to that house?" "That house" belonged to a young man who seemed to live alone except for children who appeared sometimes on weekends. My husband had spoken to him the only time we saw him in his backyard, and, though the man wasn't rude, he was evasive. It was clear he didn't want to know us or be known by us. Not knowing what kind of response a woman and a little girl would get at his doorstep, I hadn't wrapped cookies for him. I wasn't even sure I knew his name. "Why didn't we take any to that house?" Lucy wondered, and I didn't know how to answer her. I talked myself out of giving cookies when maybe his was the house that needed a whole baker's dozen.

Other times, we limit our love because we know it's not perfect. We see clearly the ways our love falls short, so we get tired and stop making the effort. "But if we love one another," 1 John tells us, "God dwells deeply within us, and his love becomes complete in us—perfect love!" (4:12). We can't know the ways others will receive our imperfect, feeble attempts at love when God intervenes. Why would we stop letting our love instincts guide us when the apostle Paul reminds us, "when the Complete arrives, our incompletes will be canceled"?[8]

Paul himself knew a thing or two about love, and he wrote about it in his first letter to the Corinthians, chapter 13. Your mind may immediately rattle off, "Love is patient, love is kind . . .," but before we consider his definition of love, let's read how he prefaces his definitions:

> If I speak with human eloquence and angelic ecstasy but don't love, I'm nothing but the creaking of a rusty gate. If I speak God's Word with power, revealing all his mysteries and making everything plain as day, and if I have faith that says to a mountain, "Jump," and it jumps, but I don't love, I'm nothing. If I give everything I own to the poor and even go to the stake to be burned as a martyr, but I don't love, I've gotten nowhere. So, no matter what I say, what I believe, and what I do, I'm bankrupt without love.

Did you catch the last part? Paul says if I don't love and I'm not going about love each day, then nothing else I do or am really matters. Period. Nothing I've done, nothing I spend my time doing or practicing for, *nothing else matters*, he says. This not only points to the heart of the gospel for those who don't follow Jesus, but also challenges the activities of those who do, making sure they guard themselves against spiritual elitism. First Corinthians 14:1 says, "Go after a life of love as if your life depended on it—because it does."

If you're like me, you'd like to be able to write an e-mail to Paul and get specifics. Perhaps you'd like to buy God a cup of coffee so that you can ask him about a particular circumstance in your life. I think we all probably agree that we should love, but our problem comes in carrying out the details. "I agree that I should love, but how does love look in this circumstance, God?" Paul understands and hopefully writes,

> We don't yet see things clearly. We're squinting in a fog, peering through a mist. But it won't be long before the weather clears and the sun shines bright! We'll see it all then, see it all as clearly as God sees us, knowing him directly just as he knows us! But for right now, until that completeness, we have three things to do to lead us toward that consummation: Trust steadily in God, hope unswervingly, love extravagantly. And the best of the three is love. (1 Cor 13:12-13)

We act as if love is a simple thing, something we check off and then move on, asking God to work some grandiose plan in our lives. "I've learned Downward-facing Dog. Now let's go to one of those really flashy yoga postures." But sometimes the root posture, the origin of our journey, becomes the method. For the Love that first captured us is not just the way, but also the truth and the life.

Practicing the Postures

1. What limits do you place on love? Pray and ask God to begin revealing them to you, and ask him to tear them away.
2. Meditate on this verse from 1 Corinthians 13:3-7: "So, no matter what I say, what I believe, and what I do, I'm bankrupt without love."

Notes

1. Gail R. O'Day, "The Gospel of John," *The New Interpreter's Bible: A Commentary in Twelve Volumes*, vol. 9 (Nashville: Abingdon Press, 1995) 750.

2. Italics mine.

3. C. Clifton Black, "The First, Second, and Third Letters of John," *The New Interpreter's Bible: A Commentary in Twelve Volumes*, vol. 12 (Nashville: Abingdon Press, 1995) 437.

4. Ibid., 433.

5. Gail R. O'Day, "The Gospel of John," *The New Interpreter's Bible: A Commentary in Twelve Volumes*, vol. 9 (Nashville: Abingdon Press, 1995) 734.

6. Black, "The First, Second, and Third Letters of John," 396.

7. Ibid., 434.

8. 1 Corinthians 13:10.